Unbeatable Chess 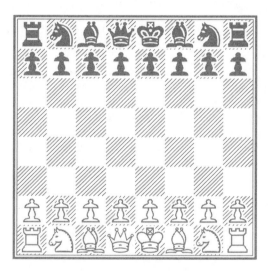 Lessons for Juniors

Instruction for the Intermediate Player

Robert M. Snyder
National Chess Master
Director of Chess for Juniors

Random House
Puzzles & Games

This book is available for special purchases in bulk by organizations and institutions,
not for resale, at special discounts. Please direct your inquiries to
Random House Premium Sales, fax 212-572-4961.

Please address inquiries about electronic licensing of reference products, for use on
a network or in software or on CD-ROM, to the Subsidiary Rights Department,
Random House Information Group, fax 212-940-7352.

Visit the Random House Puzzles & Games Web site: www.puzzlesatrandom.com

Typeset and printed in the United States of America.

Library of Congress Cataloging-in-Publication Data is available.

First Edition

0 9 8 7 6 5 4 3 2 1

ISBN: 0-8129-3511-X

Acknowledgments

Thanks are due to Calvin Olson and Charles Sendrey for their assistance in proofreading and reviewing the original manuscript.

*To my National Champions
who have inspired me to write
a more advanced book.*

Introduction

When I wrote my first major chess book, *Chess For Juniors*, over a decade ago, I had no idea that it would turn out to be one of the bestselling chess books of all time. I personally was in need of a good chess book to introduce the basics of chess to my beginning students. And, it was perhaps this motivating idea that made *Chess For Juniors* a success.

After many years of urging by my readers for a second, more advanced book, I decided to put together a book based on games that I personally use in lessons with my students. I have selected these games first and foremost for their instructive value. However, I have also selected games that I feel are interesting and will provide an element of beauty for entertainment purposes. It has been said that chess is a sport, science and art. Any good chess teacher must take all three of these factors into consideration when giving lessons.

Unbeatable Chess Lessons For Juniors, though directed at the intermediate-level scholastic player, is a book for any player who knows the basics, regardless of age. I use a tiered approach in each lesson. Basic ideas are reviewed to make sure nothing is missed while going into more detailed analysis and concepts. Every move in each game is commented on. However, if the same moves appear in an earlier game, the same comments will not be repeated.

A great variety of tactical ideas, positional concepts and openings are covered in these games. Games were selected that contain instructive elements at

all phases, but without a large focus on the endgame. Many of the games are played by some of the world's most famous players. However, since a teacher understands his/her own games best, I have included a large number of my own games. A little background on some of the more famous players and a brief description of each game at the beginning makes the games more interesting.

With the exception of a review of basic symbols used in this book, I have not included a primer covering notation, rules or basic strategy, as these were all covered in *Chess For Juniors*. However, as mentioned, I will review basic ideas in the analysis when I feel they are important. So if you only have a basic knowledge of chess, don't feel that this book may be too advanced for you. When the names of the players in a game are shown, the first player named, which is on the left, is playing White. Now, let's get into our first lesson!

Contents

Symbols Used in This Book

Symbol	Meaning
x	captures
+	check
++	checkmate
=	promoted to a
0-0	castles Kingside
0-0-0	castles Queenside
e.p.	en passant
?	weak move
??	very weak move (a blunder)
!	strong move
!!	very strong move

My Favorite Game

Hamppe versus Meitner
Vienna, 1872

Opening: Vienna Game

This, by far, is my favorite game. When I go over this game with my students I call it the "King-Hunt Game". It is just awesome! White sacrifices a piece to expose the White King to attack. Then to keep the attack alive, he continues to feed the fire by sacrificing more and more material! While the White King is driven across the board, the final result doesn't become clear until the end. The slightest inaccuracy by either side can have a fatal result.

1 e4

I recommend playing 1 e4 to all my beginning and intermediate level students. It takes a firm foothold in the center, while freeing a Bishop and Queen. It offers beginning and intermediate players the widest variety of tactical and positional opportunities of any first move for learning purposes.

1...e5

I also recommend playing 1...e5 to my students for all the same reasons as playing 1 e4.

2 Nc3

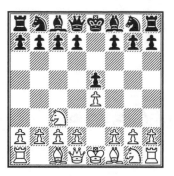

Diagram 1. Position after 2 Nc3

This move usually leads to the Vienna Game opening. It is less aggressive than playing 2 Nf3, but it is a sound developing move that defends the "e" pawn.

2...Bc5

The general rule, *"It is better to develop Knights before Bishops,"* applies here. Though 2...Bc5 is not a blunder, I would recommend going into the main line of the Vienna Opening with 2...Nf6, which is played in Lesson 3. This may continue with the aggressive 3 f4 d5 4 fxe5 Nxe4, resulting in an equal game.

3 Na4

A strange move forcing Black to make a decision about his attacked Bishop on "c5". It is awkward to place a Knight on the edge of the board so early in the game. The saying, "A Knight on the rim is dim, its chances are very slim" certainly does apply here. It would have been better to develop another piece with 3 Nf3. The only reason there is any soundness to Black's Bishop sacrifice on the next move is because of White's exposed Knight on "a4". This will become apparent later in the game.

3...Bxf2 +

This exposes the King to an interesting attack. At the beginning of the game the "f2" and "f7" squares are only defended by a King. This makes these two squares the most vulnerable points of attack on the board. However, Black could have simply played 3...Be7. This still leaves White's Knight awkwardly posted on the edge of the board.

4 Kxf2

White must accept the sacrifice. The only other legal move, 4 Ke2, would leave White a Pawn down and his King would still be exposed.

4...Qh4+

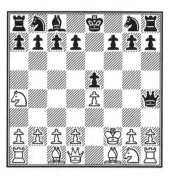

Diagram 2. Position after 4...Qh4+

Black's Queen attacks both the King and White's unprotected "e" Pawn. After having sacrificed a piece Black must play aggressively, otherwise White will have time to get his King into safety. If Black played 4...Qf6+?, White could simply make a constructive developing move with 5 Nf3 or offer a Queen trade with 5 Qf3. In either case Black's attack would come to a standstill. As a general rule, *"When you are ahead in material or if your opponent has an attack, it is good to make even exchanges of pieces."*

5 Ke3

This is the only move to avoid immediate disaster. If 5 g3? then 5...Qxe4 forking the Knight and Rook. If 5 Kf3? then 5...d5!, and White cannot meet Black's many threats such as a skewer with 6...Bg4+ or fork with 6...Qxe4+.

5...Qf4+

Black keeps the initiative by driving White's King to "d3" where he blocks his own "d" Pawn and Bishop. Black aims, through continuous threats, to not give White time to get his King into safety.

6 Kd3

Forced, since 6 Ke2? allows 6...Qe4+ forking King and Knight.

6…d5

Diagram 3. Position after 6…d5

What I like about this game is its instructive elements of both attack and defense. Black is threatening 6…Qxe4+.

Take a good look at this position and see if you can find White's best defense here without looking at the next move in the game.

7 Kc3!

It is better to be a live chicken and run than to try and hold onto the "e" Pawn and become a dead duck! Many of my students stubbornly try to defend the "e" Pawn here with moves like 7 Nc3 dxe4+ 8 Nxe4, which allows a killer pin after 8…Bf5. Then, if White tries defending the Knight with 9 Qf3 Black, wins easily after 9…Bxe4+ 10 Qxe4 Qxf1+.

7…Qxe4

Getting a second Pawn for his sacrificed piece and threatening the Knight on "a4".

8 Kb3

Defending his Knight while trying to seek safety on the Queenside.

8…Na6

Black develops his Knight with the threat of 9…Qb4++. However, 8…Nc6 developing toward the center would have been better.

9 a3

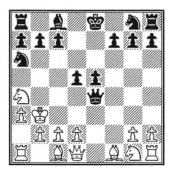

Diagram 4. Position after 9 a3

White defends against the mate threat and opens up "a2" as a possible hiding place for his King. If given an extra move here White would play 10 Nc3 and then the King can hide on "a2" whenever he wants. However, White could have done even better by giving up a Pawn with 9 d4! exd4 10 Bxa6 bxa6 12 Nc5 and White's King is safe after 12...Rb8+ 13 Ka3.

See if you can find Black's best move here without looking at the next move in the game.

9...Qxa4+

Black embarks on a risky sacrifice to keep his attack alive. Black did not like any of the alternatives. If he tried opening up a diagonal for Black's Bishop to attack from e6 with 9...d4 then White could hide his King with 10 Ka2.

10 Kxa4

White must accept the sacrifice. This is no time to be a chicken! If 10 Ka2, then Black would be two Pawns ahead and would win easily.

10...Nc5+

Black must prevent White's King from getting to "b3" where he could then hide on "a2".

11 Kb4?

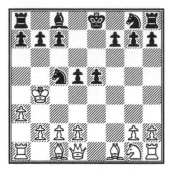

Diagram 5. Position after 11 Kb4

White overlooks 11 Kb5!. White could defend and eventually escape in all variations. For example, if Black played 11...b6 White could return some of the material with a winning game after 12 d4 exd4 13 Qxd4 Ne7 14 Qxc5!. Or if 11...a5 then White is winning after 12 b4! Ne7 13 bxa5!.

11...a5+!

Black must offer yet another piece to keep his attack alive! Otherwise, if given an extra move, White could play 12 a4, opening up an easy escape square for his King on a3.

12 Kxc5

White has nothing better than to accept more material! If White refuses the material and tries for a win with 12 Kc3 the game might continue 12...d4+ 13 Kc4 b6 14 Qf3 Be6+ 15 Qd5 Bxd5+ 16 Kxd5 Nf6+! and Black's two Pawns and great position easily compensate for the piece.

12...Ne7

Defending the "d" Pawn and threatening mate in two moves with either 13...b6+ 14 Kb5 Bd7++, or 13...Bd7 followed by 14...b6++.

13 Bb5+

White must counter attack aggressively to stay alive! This sets up White's next move to prevent a quick mate.

13...Kd8

Diagram 6. Position after 13...Kd8

Black threatens 14...b6++. See if you can find the only move to prevent mate.

14 Bc6!

This uses the motif known as "interference". White blocks out Black's ability to attack White's King along the "e8-a4" diagonal with his Bishop.

14...b6+

Black continues his attack on Black's King, as he cannot give White a moment to breathe. Otherwise, White's overwhelming material advantage will win easily.

15 Kb5

The only legal move! I did promise a comment to every move in every game!

15...Nxc6

Diagram 7. Position after 15...Nxc6

Black now threatens 16...Nd4+ 17 Ka4 Bd7++ as well as simply 16...Bd7 followed by Nd4++.

I ask my students here, "Should you eat (16 Kxc6) or head toward home and retreat (16 Ka4)?" What is your answer?

16 Kxc6

The answer is simple. Eat or die! If 16 Ka4? then White could not prevent mate after 16...Nd4! with both 17...Bd7++ and 17...b5++ threatened. White now threatens to have his King escape with 17 Kxd5.

16...Bb7+!

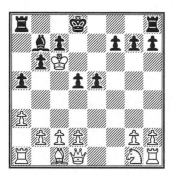

Diagram 8. Position after 16...Bb7+!

Black offers to feed the White King more! Should you eat or retreat? What would you do here?

17 Kb5

White makes a wise choice! Taking the Bishop with 17 Kxb7 would be a fatal mistake. Black would play 17...Kd7 with Rhb8++ to follow.

17...Ba6+

Once again, Black cannot give White any time to breathe! Otherwise, White's overwhelming material advantage will come into play.

18 Kc6

If White's King tries to escape with 18 Ka4??, then Black traps the King with 18...Bc4!, and 19...b5++ follows!

18...Bb7+

Here the players agreed to a draw, as the position is soon to repeat itself three times. If either side deviates from repeating moves, a loss is guaranteed!

l e s s o n

2

Taking Advantage
of a Weak Opening

Snyder (USA) versus Blank (Israel)
10th ICCF Correspondence Olympics, 1977–1978

Opening: Vienna Game

Black's second move creates a hole on "d5". White takes full advantage of it by first posting a Knight and then a Bishop in the hole! Planning ahead for an effective use of Pawns and pieces is demonstrated to combat a fixed Pawn formation. Black's tactical blunders at the end bring about an abrupt finish.

1 e4 e5 2 Nc3 c5?

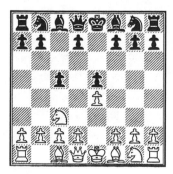

Diagram 9. Position after 2...c5

This creates a hole on "d5" which White will take full advantage of. A "hole" is a square that has enemy Pawns on the adjacent squares beside and behind it. This makes a hole a natural outpost for enemy pieces since a piece occupying the hole cannot be driven away by enemy Pawns.

Black also fixes his Pawn formation early in the game, which cuts down on his options. The Pawn on "c5" also restricts Black's Bishop on "f8". Better would have been 2...Nf6 as recommended in LESSON ONE and played in LESSON THREE.

3 Bc4

This is a very effective location for White's Bishop. The Bishop is placed on the long "a2-g8" diagonal attacking the hole on "d5" and Black's weak square on "f7". White's plan of freeing and developing his pieces along with a plan to attack Black's Pawn center will give White a nice advantage.

3...Nf6

You will see that Black plays very aggressively in this opening. Black develops and tries to challenge White's control over the "d5" square. However, either 3...d6, freeing the Bishop on "c8" and defending his Pawns, or 3...Nc6 developing his Knight, would have been good alternatives.

4 d3

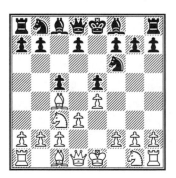

Diagram 10. Position after 4 d3

White frees his Bishop on "c1" and defends his "e" Pawn and Bishop on "c4". Though developing his Knight with 4 Nf3 looks natural, White doesn't want to block his "f" Pawn. White's plans to attack Black's fixed center Pawns with his "f" Pawn. There is another plan that White could have considered which uses his Pawns to attack Black's Pawn center. White could post his Knight on "d5" and then play moves like c3 and d4. However, this plan would be very time consuming, and White would still need to protect his "e" Pawn before embarking on such a plan.

4...d6

Black frees his Bishop on "c8" and defends his center Pawns.

5 f4

White follows through on his plan to attack Black's center with his "f" Pawn. When White castles Kingside, note that his Rook will end up on the "f" file, increasing attacking chances on that side of the board.

5...Bg4

Black plays aggressively, attacking White's Queen. It is difficult to find a good square for this Bishop. Therefore, it would have been better to delay its development. As a general rule *"It is better to make the least committing moves first."* I was expecting Black to either play 5...Be7 developing his other Bishop to its only available square, or 5...Nc6 developing his Knight to its most natural post.

6 Nf3

White develops his Knight to its most natural square while blocking Black's attack on the Queen.

6...Nc6

Diagram 11. Position after 6...Nc6

Black develops his Knight to its most natural square. His plan is to play 7...Nd4 and then capture on "f3" forcing White to play gxf3 closing off White's "f" file and breaking up his Kingside Pawns.

Without looking at the next move in the game, see if you can find what White's move was that stopped Black's plan.

7 h3!

Correct timing! This forces White's Bishop to either capture on f3 or retreat to an inferior square. Therefore, Black will have no time to continue with his previously mentioned plan.

7...Bxf3

Black has nothing better than to give up his Bishop pair. As a general rule, *"Bishops are slightly better than Knights in open positions."* Black doesn't like the idea of retreating the Bishop. If 7...Be6 Black gets doubled isolated pawns after 8 Bxe6 fxe6 9 fxe5 Nxe5 10 Nxe5 dxe5. If 7...Bh5?, then the Bishop would be trapped after 8 g4 Bg6 9 f5. If 7...Bd7? Black must lose a Pawn after 8 Ng5.

8 Qxf3

Recovering the piece and bringing the Queen actively into play.

8...Nd4

White doesn't mind allowing Black's Knight to have the d4 outpost. Eventually the Knight can be driven away by White's "c" Pawn.

9 Qf2

The Queen gets out of attack while going to another active post. She covers the second rank and will help exert pressure along the potentially open "f" file.

9...Be7

Diagram 12. Position after 9...Be7

This completes his minor piece development and prepares to castle.

10 Nd5

This move posts the Knight actively and takes advantage of the hole on "d5". This was the more aggressive choice. Getting the King into safety and out of the center with 10 0-0 would have been a reasonable alternative.

10...b5

Black also plays actively attacking the Bishop and trying to obtain counterplay on the Queenside. If Black played 10...Nxd5 then White's Bishop would be strongly posted in the hole after 11 Bxd5 attacking the unprotected "b" Pawn and threatening 12 fxe5 with a discovered attack on "f7".

11 Nxf6+

White's only good plan. White doesn't have a good square for his attacked Bishop so he clears "d5". Very weak would be 11 Bb3 as Black would not hesitate to play 11...Nxb3 and White no longer has the Bishop pair.

11...Bxf6

This is the only good way to recapture the piece. If 11...gxf6 12 Bd5 Black has a very bad Bishop on "e7", his doubled Pawns are weak, and his King would be exposed if he castled on either side.

12 Bd5

Diagram 13. Position after 12 Bd5

He now occupies the hole on "d5" with attack on Black's Rook. The Bishop is now on a very strong central post.

12...Rc8

Black gets his Rook out of attack while covering the important "c6" square. Weak would have been 12...Rb8?, because Black would have lost his ability to castle after 13 c3 Ne6 14 Bc6+.

13 fxe5

Correct timing! White opens up the "f" file and pins Black's Bishop on "f6". If White played 12 c3 first, then Black could have obtained counterplay after 12...Nc6 13 fxe5? Nxe5 threatening White's weakened "d" Pawn with 14...Nxd3+.

13...dxe5

This is Black's only way to recover the Pawn. Black cannot play 13...Bxe5?? because of 14 Qxf7++.

14 0-0

White gets his King out of the center and into safety while bringing his Rook onto the open "f" file. You will see later in the game how useful the pressure on the "f" file

becomes. Some of my students while analyzing this game have suggested the tempting 14 Bg5, attacking Black's pinned Bishop. This is a big mistake, as White's Queen would become an overworked defender by trying to defend the "c" Pawn and pin Black's Bishop at the same time. Black could then win a Pawn by playing 14...Nxc2+ 15 Qxc2 Bxg5. However, after 14 0-0 playing 15 Bg5 becomes a threat.

14...0-0

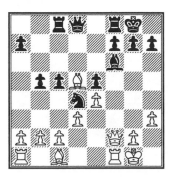

Diagram 14. Position after 14...0-0

Black also gets his King into safety and out of the center. This also helps protect the "f7" square, which is important due to White's strong pressure along the "f" file.

15 c3

White finally drives Black's Knight back from its active post. This also relieves White's Queen from being tied down to the defense of the "c" Pawn.

15...Ne6

Black gets his Knight out of attack while defending his "c" Pawn.

16 Be3

White develops his last minor piece and threatens to win Black's "c" Pawn. White's plan of simple development, taking advantage of Black's weakness on the "d5" square and favorably opening up lines has paid off. White stands better in the center and on both sides of the board due to having the Bishop pair, pressure along the "f" file and a threat of winning Black's "c" Pawn with 17 Bxe6 fxe6 18 Bxc5.

It would have been a mistake to double Black's Pawns at this point with 16 Bxe6. After 16...fxe6 Black obtains some counterplay by having his "f" file opened and White having a backward "d" Pawn on an open file.

16...Bg5?

Diagram 15. Position after 14...Bg5

Black's concept of trading his less active Bishop for White's more active Bishop is good. However, this is a tactical blunder that should cost him at least a Pawn. Black should have played 16...Qe7 defending his "c" Pawn, bringing his Queen into play and connecting his Rooks. After 16...Qe7 White can tie down Black's Bishop to the defense of the "e" Pawn with 17 Qf5. This would hinder Black's ability to get his Bishop to "g5".

See if you can find White's best move here without looking at the next move in the book.

17 Bxe6

This forces the win of at least a Pawn by removing the Knight's defense of the Bishop on "g5" and opening up the "f" file.

17...fxe6??

This is a second tactical blunder, which loses a piece instead of a Pawn. Black's Queen now becomes an overworked defender, trying to defend the Rook on "f8" and Bishop on "g5". Black thought that White had to move his Queen, overlooking White's next move. Black would have lost only a Pawn had he played 17...Bxe3 18 Bxf7+ Rxf7 19 Qxe3.

18 Qxf8+!

Black resigned. Black's Queen must abandon the Bishop on "g5" after 18...Qxf8 19 Rxf8+ Kxf8 20 Bxg5 and White would be a full piece ahead.

Planning Ahead

Snyder (USA) versus Schmeleff (Australia)
ICCF Master Class Tournament, 1977–1979

Opening: Vienna Game

This game shows the importance of planning ahead for the endgame. White uses a combination on move nine to get the Bishop pair and better Pawn structure. Then Black makes the game interesting by sacrificing a Pawn to get active piece play and to increase his drawing chances by having Bishops of opposite colors. With careful and meticulous play, White neutralizes Black's counterplay, and uses an extra Pawn and better Pawn structure to bring home victory.

1 e4 e5 2 Nc3 Nf6

Diagram 16. Position after 2...Nf6

This is considered to be Black's best and most active move against the Vienna Game. He develops a Knight with immediate pressure on White's "e" Pawn. With 2...Nf6 Black is also supporting a possible 3...d5.

3 g3

White prepares to fianchetto his bishop to "g2", where it will back up White's "e" Pawn to exert pressure in the center. This is considered to be a rather conservative and positional way of playing the Vienna Opening. Other common moves here are 3 f4, as mentioned in LESSON ONE, or 3 Bc4 where Black has the choice of simple development with 3...Nc6 or heading toward complications with 3...Nxe4 4 Qh5 (if 4 Nxe4 then Black gets his piece back with 4...d5, forking the Knight and Bishop) Nd6.

3...d5

This is an aggressive move, which boldly attacks in the center and opens up lines for both sides. Other reasonable but less active developing moves are either 3...Bc5 or 3...Nc6.

4 exd5

White relieves the pressure on his "e" Pawn by exchanging it for Black's Pawn and he opens up the "h1"-"a8" diagonal for future use by his Bishop. It would have been a mistake to try to defend the "e" Pawn with 4 Bg2. White's Bishop would become poorly placed and a target in the center after 4...dxe4 5 Nxe4 Nxe4 6 Bxe4 Bc5. Here Black has the neat threat of 7...Bxf2+ 8 Kxf2 Qd4+.

4...Nxd5

Black recovers his Pawn and brings his Knight actively into the center.

5 Bg2

Diagram 17. Position after 5 Bg2

White finally completes his fianchetto and threatens Black's Knight on "d5".

5...Be6?

Black develops his Bishop while defending his Knight on "d5". Until this game was played many opening books considered 5...Be6 to be the best move. Now 5...Nxc3 6 bxc3 Bd6 is considered a better line, which leads to a roughly equal game with active play for both sides.

6 Nf3

White develops his Knight toward the center and attacks Black's "e" Pawn. White's main plan is to apply pressure to Black's "e" Pawn with both his Knight and his Rook along the "e" file.

6...Nc6

Black develops his Knight toward the center defending his attacked "e" Pawn.

7 0-0

White gets his King out of the center and into safety while preparing to bring his Rook to the "e" file.

7...Be7

Black completes his minor piece development and prepares to also castle.

8 Re1

White brings his Rook onto the open "e" file, continuing with his plan of putting pressure on Black's weak "e" Pawn.

8 . . . Bf6

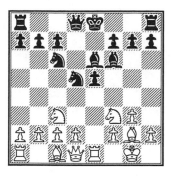

Diagram 18. Position after 8...Bf6

This defends Black's threatened "e" Pawn.

9 Nxd5!

White forces Black's Bishop to recapture, which puts a pin on Black's "e" Pawn. This will allow White to continue his build up on the Pawn even further. The opening books written before this game was played showed only 9 Ne4 as the recommended move, but this blocks White's attack along the "e" file. I had prepared this opening improvement for an important tournament game and actually got to use it twice before it was published.

9 . . . Bxd5

This is the only decent way of recapturing the piece. Black would have lost a Pawn immediately if he played 9...Qxd5. White would then play 10 Nxe5, with a discovered attack on the Black Queen by the Bishop on "g2".

10 d4

Diagram 19. Position after 10 d4

This is the point of White's previous move. White boldly strikes at the center, freeing his Bishop and attacking Black's pinned "e" Pawn a third time. Black now has the uncomfortable decision of determining what to do about his threatened "e" Pawn.

10...e4

In this game Black decides to temporarily relieve some of the pressure on his "e" Pawn by advancing it. He hopes to trade it for White's "d" Pawn; however, Black will soon discover that he is simply trading one problem for another!

My other game using this opening line was against Fritz Oppenrieder, the former Correspondence Chess Champion of Germany. He decided to immediately give up his Bishop pair with 10...Bxf3. The game continued, 11 Bxf3 Nxd4 12 Bxb7 Rb8 13 Bg2 0-0 14 c3 Nb5 (If 14...Ne6?, then 15 Qa4! and Black's "a" Pawn is lost) 15 Be3 and White eventually won due to his several advantages: the Bishop pair, better Pawn structure and Queenside Pawn majority.

As a general rule, *"Having a majority of Pawns on the Queenside is an advantage if both players have castled Kingside."* This is because in the middlegame the side with the Queenside Pawn majority can advance the Queenside Pawns without exposing his castled King. In the endgame the side with the Queenside Pawn majority has the enemy King farther away from interfering with the advance of the Queenside Pawns or stopping the advance of a potential passed Pawn.

11 Nd2

This will allow Black to exchange his weak "e" Pawn for White's "d" Pawn. However, White is setting up a combination to obtain the Bishop pair and give Black doubled isolated Pawns. I looked at 11 c3 with the idea of first defending the "d" Pawn and planning to meet 11...0-0 with 12 Nd2 winning Black's "e" Pawn. Then I noticed that Black has a defensive resource after 11 c3. He could play 11...Be7, shielding his King and planning to meet 12 Nd2 with 12...f5, defending his "e" Pawn. White's game would have been good here, but 11 Nd2 gives White a bigger advantage.

11...Bxd4

Black has no choice but to capture the Pawn before White defends it. If Black gets his King out of the center with 11...0-0, then White would win Black's "e" Pawn after 12 c3.

12 Nxe4

This recovers White's Pawn and threatens a killer discovered check with 13 Nf6+.

12...0-0

Black gets his King out of the center and into safety, avoiding White's threatened discovered check.

13 c3

This will drive away Black's Bishop from its center post, setting up the neat combination that follows.

13...Bb6

Diagram 20. Position after 13...Bb6

If Black had seen White's combination he would have realized it would have been better to give up the Bishop pair right away with 13...Bxe4 14 Bxe4 Bb6 15 Bf4. White would have a nice advantage here but this would have been the lesser of the evils.

See if you can find White's best move here without looking at the next move in the game. You have already received some hints!

14 Qxd5!

This is a temporary Queen sacrifice that sets up a discovered attack, which will leave Black with doubled isolated Pawns and White with the Bishop pair.

14...Qxd5

Black was forced to take White's Queen; otherwise he would be a Bishop down.

15 Nf6+

This move recovers White's Queen by putting Black's King in check with the Knight uncovering an attack on the Black Queen by the Bishop on "g2".

15...gxf6

Once again another forced move for Black; otherwise the Knight would escape capture! Black now gets doubled isolated Pawns. As a general rule *"Doubled Pawns are considered a weakness as they cannot protect each other and the Pawn in the front often blocks the movement of the Pawn behind it."* However, sometimes there are some good points to keep in mind about doubled Pawns. As another general rule *"When you get doubled Pawns an open file is created that might be useful for a rook, and some-*

times capturing toward the center will help make your center stronger." Unfortunately for Black, in the case of this game, none of these good points will be useful to him.

16 Bxd5

Diagram 21. Position after 16 Bxd5

White recovers his Queen. The Bishop is also actively posted in the center. Black must now concern himself about the possibility of White playing 17 Bxc6 giving Black yet another set of doubled isolated Pawns. In such a case every one of Black's Pawns would also be isolated and Black could not hope to survive the endgame.

16...Ne5

This is Black's best practical chance to get counterplay. Black is willing to give up a Pawn to activate his Knight and get all of his pieces into play.

17 Bxb7

White accepts Black's Pawn sacrifice, isolates Black's Queenside Pawns and threatens Black's Rook on "a8". Now all of Black's Pawns are isolated! As a general rule *"An isolated Pawn is a weakness because the Pawn can only be defended by pieces, and not by other Pawns."*

17...Rad8

Black gets his Rook out of attack while placing it on an open file. Black's Knight is very active. It has potential attacking posts on "d3" and "g4". The Knight also ties down White's Bishop to the defense of "f3".

18 Kg2

Diagram 22. Position after 18 Kg2

This helps to consolidate White's position by covering "f3" with the King, unpinning the "f" Pawn and removing the King from a possibly exposed first rank. The natural-looking developing move 18 Be3 is very weak because of 18...Rb8 19 Bg2 Bxe3 20 Rxe3 Rxb2, and Black has recovered his Pawn and has a Rook actively posted on the 7th rank.

18...Nd3

Posting the Knight on a very active post threatening White's Rook and "f" Pawn.

19 Re2

White keeps his Rook as active as possible while getting it out of attack and defending his "f" Pawn.

19...Rfe8

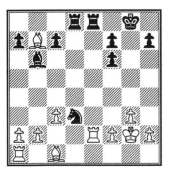

Diagram 23. Position after 19...Rfe8

Black brings his last piece into play, attacking White's Rook on the "e" file.

20 Be3

White finally develops his Bishop, frees his Rook on "a1" and blocks out Black's Rook on the "e" file.

20...Rb8?

Black removes his Rook from a stronger file because of false hopes of getting play against White's "b" Pawn. Black would have done better to give White an isolated "e" Pawn with 20...Bxe3. However, after 21 fxe3 Black cannot win his Pawn back with 21...Rb8, because White counters with 22 Rd1!, attacking Black's Knight.

21 Ba6

White gets his Bishop out of attack while attacking Black's unprotected Knight on "d3".

21...Bxe3

Black hopes to get drawing chances by making exchanges that lead to a Bishops of opposite color endgame. As a general rule *"Endgames with Bishops of opposite colors tend to be much more likely to be a draw than endgames with Bishops on the same color."* This is because the player with the material advantage is: 1) not able to use his Bishop to challenge the other player's Bishop and force an exchange of Bishops, 2) sometimes not able to prevent his Pawns from being blockaded by the combined use of the enemy King and Bishop, and 3) unable to attack and win any Pawns defended by the enemy Bishop. However, as you will see in this case Black's Pawn structure is so weak that even a Bishops of opposite color endgame will not save him.

22 Bxd3

This recovers the piece while removing Black's very actively posted Knight and leaving Black's Bishop under attack.

22...Bc5

Diagram 24. Position after 22...Bc5

Black gets his Bishop out of attack while maintaining as much activity for his pieces as possible.

When I use this game in their lessons, here is where I ask my students to find the best plan for White. See if you can find White's best move here without looking at the next move in the game.

23 Rxe8+!

White lets Black have control of the "e" file. In this case the "d" file is the more important file to control. The key here is the 7th rank. Along the "e" file both sides have Bishops, which can possibly control the "e2" and "e7" squares on their side of the board and can possibly prevent the Rooks from penetrating to their respective 7th ranks. Since the Bishops cannot possibly control the "d2" and "d7" squares on their side of the board the player who controls the "d" file in this game controls the more important file. Gee, isn't chess logical!

23...Rxe8

This is Black's only move to recover his Rook.

24 Rd1

White takes command of the open "d" file. White's Bishop may be in the way of the Rook for now, but this is only temporary.

24...a5

Black wants to restrain White from playing "b4" and advancing his Queenside Pawns. However, the drawback to this is that Black's Pawn on "a5" is easier to attack. In reality Black is lost at this point, and sometimes playing aggressively instead of sitting back and allowing the opponent to come and get you is your best practical chance.

White could not have challenged Black with his Rook on the "d" file at this point with 24...Rd8??, because of 25 Bxh7+ Kxh7 26 Rxd8.

25 Bc4

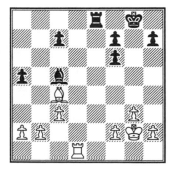

Diagram 25. Position after 25 Bc4

White opens up the "d" file for his Rook and attacks Black's weak Pawn on "f7". White would like to penetrate with his Rook to the 7th rank.

25...Re4

Black plays actively and attacks White's Bishop. White must now make a decision on how to handle the threat.

26 Bb5

This gets the Bishop out of attack while maintaining control over the "e2" square. A move like 26 Bb3? would allow White's Rook to penetrate with 26...Re2 attacking White's "b" and "f" Pawns. Playing 26 b3 would have maintained the Bishop on the good "a2-g8" diagonal; however, White is trying to avoid placing his Pawns on the same color as his Bishop. This would increase Black's chances of blockading White's Queenside Pawns. As a general rule *"You should place your Pawns on the opposite color of your Bishop."*

26...Re6

Black continues to try to get counterplay. His idea is to play 27...Rb6 attacking and pinning White's Bishop.

27 Rd5

White attacks Black's Bishop. This will either force Black's Bishop to retreat to a less desirable location, or to defend the Bishop with his Rook.

27...Re5

Black offers a trade of Rooks while defending his Bishop.

28 Rd7

White penetrates to the 7th rank with his Rook attacking Black's "c" and "f" Pawns. As a general rule, *"The 7th rank is a great attacking location for a Rook."* White did not want to trade Rooks at this point with 28 Rxe5 because Black would then undouble his Pawns with 28...fxe5.

28...Re7

Black does not want to allow White's Rook to control the 7th rank, so he challenges it. If Black played 28...Bxf2 with a discovered attack on White's Bishop, White has the strong reply, 29 Bc4, getting the Bishop out of attack. White would then be threatening Black's Bishop and Pawns on "c7" and "f7".

29 Rxe7

White now exchanges Rooks on his terms. Black's Bishop is forced to retreat to a less active diagonal when recapturing.

29...Bxe7

Diagram 26. Position after 29...Bxe7

This is Black's only move to recover the Rook. White realizes that this Bishops of opposite color endgame is clearly won.

White's plan consists of the following ideas (not necessarily in the exact order that they are carried out):

1. White will make sure that his Kingside Pawns are secure against any threats by Black's Bishop. This may require placing the Kingside Pawns on the same color as his Bishop which may be a drawback; however, it will prevent Black's Bishop from attacking them in the absence of White's King.

2. White will move his King toward Black's weak isolated Queenside Pawns. The King can easily threaten them from the White squares and can aid in the creation and support of a White Queenside passed Pawn.

3. When White's King has reached the Queenside, White plans to create a passed "a" Pawn by placing his Pawn on "b4". This would force Black to exchange or lose his "a" Pawn.

4. White's Bishop will be used to restrain any activity by Black's Pawns on either side of the Board. If any of these isolated Pawns go to a White square, they can easily be attacked by White's Bishop. Note that Black's King is already restricted to the defense of the weak Pawn on "f7". If Black's King heads toward the Queenside to aid his weak Pawns there, then White's Bishop can attack and win Black's Pawn on "f7". Therefore, Black has the choice of losing another Pawn or having a King that cannot aid matters on the Queenside.

30 f4

This prepares to bring White's King toward the Queenside. If White had played the natural looking 30 Kf3 then Black could temporarily restrain White's King by attacking his "f" Pawn with 30...Bc5. White realizes that sooner or later his "f" Pawn will need to be advanced due to a future attack by Black's dark squared Bishop.

30...Bc5

Black brings his Bishop back onto the more active "g1-a7" diagonal, where he has hopes of getting counterplay against White's Kingside Pawns.

31 Kf3

White's King begins his plan of heading toward Black's Queenside Pawns.

31...Kf8

Black's King now heads toward a more active central location where he can make the choice of going to the Queenside, which gives up his "f" Pawn, or staying near his "f" Pawn to protect it against White's Bishop.

32 Ke4

The White King continues his journey toward Black's Queenside Pawns.

32...Ke7

Diagram 27. Position after 32...Ke7

Black's King follows through with his plan of becoming as centralized as possible.

33 f5

This completely restrains Black's doubled "f" Pawns while starting to get White's Pawns off the dark squares. If White immediately continued with his plan of bringing his King toward the Queenside with 33 Kd5 then Black would win one of White's Kingside Pawns after 33...Bg1 34 h3 Bh2. As a general rule, *"When you are clearly winning do not take a risky or complicated path when you have a clear way of winning that avoids risk or complications."* On the other hand Black, who is losing at this point, would like to complicate matters.

33...Bg1

Black begins his attack on White's Pawns so they become fixed and difficult to use in a possible breakthrough on the Kingside. However, Black's best practical chance

was to play 33...Kd6, using the King as an active fighting piece and keeping White's King out of "d5". In other words, Black should have made the choice of giving up his weak "f7" Pawn. If Black had played 33...Kd6, then White could play 34 a3 with the plan of eventually getting a Passed Pawn by moving his Pawn to "b4".

34 h3

This gets White's "h" Pawn out of attack.

34...Bf2

Black continues his attack on White's Kingside Pawns while trying to reposition his Bishop to attack White's Queenside Pawns.

35 g4

This gets White's "g" Pawn out of attack.

35...Be1

Black is maneuvering his Bishop toward the Queenside to try to attack and re-strain White's Pawns there. However, once again Black's best practical chance was to use his King actively and play 35...Kd6.

36 Kd5

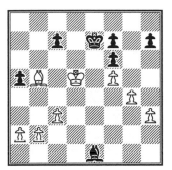

Diagram 28. Position after 36 Kd5

White's King continues his plan of heading toward Black's Queenside Pawns.

36...Bd2

Black positions his Bishop to be able to possibly attack White's "b" Pawn.

37 a4

White advances his "a" Pawn, which will soon become a Passed Pawn and bring home victory! White now threatens 38 b4, forcing a Passed "a" Pawn, which cannot be stopped.

37...Bc1

At this point there is really nothing for Black to do. This threatens White's "b" Pawn, which he planned to move anyway.

38 b4

This gets the "b" Pawn out of danger while attacking Black's "a" Pawn. As a result White's "a" Pawn will become an Outside Passed Pawn.

38...axb4

Black exchanges off his "a" Pawn since there was no way of defending it.

39 cxb4

Diagram 29. Position after 39 cxb4

Recovering the Pawn.

39...Be3

Black covers the "a7" square, which White's "a" Pawn must get past in order to become a Queen. However, it really doesn't matter! When White's King gets to "b7" to support the Pawn, Black must give up his Bishop for it.

40 Kc6

White begins his King march to "b7" which will support the advance of the passed "a" Pawn.

40...Kd8

Black defends his "c" Pawn, which is really of no interest to White at this point.

41 Kb7

Diagram 30. Position after 41 Kb7

White's King now will support the "a" Pawn and block Black's King's entrance to the Queenside.

41 ... Bd2

Attacking the unprotected "b" Pawn, which does nothing to stop the advance of White's "a" Pawn. However, Black had nothing better to do.

42 a5

Black resigned. White will advance his "a" Pawn, forcing Black to give up his Bishop for it on "a7".

Opening Up Lines against the Castled King

Jose Capablanca versus Herman Steiner
Los Angeles, 1933

Opening: Four Knights Game

Capablanca was the World Champion from 1921 to 1927. For a long time he was considered to be the perfect chess machine. From 1916 to 1924 he didn't lose a single tournament or match game! He defeated Emanuel Lasker decisively in a World Championship match in 1921 after Lasker had resigned the title to him the previous year. However, Capablanca wanted to prove himself and insisted on playing a formal match for the title. In 1927 Capablanca lost his title to Alexander Alekhine who never gave him a chance for a return match.

Herman Steiner was an International Master who lived in California and was the chess columnist for the *Los Angeles Times* newspaper.

In this game White strips Black's Castled King of his Pawn shield and opens up the "f" file for his Rook. After Capablanca makes a deeply calculated Rook sacrifice, the King hunt begins!

1 e4 e5 2 Nf3

Diagram 31. Position after 2 Nf3

This is by far the most common move played in this position. White develops his Knight toward the center with an immediate attack on Black's "e" Pawn.

2...Nc6

This is the most common response by Black. Black develops his Knight toward the center and defends his "e" Pawn.

3 Nc3

White develops another Knight toward the center and defends his "e" Pawn. This simple developing move is very sound. However, it has never been as popular as playing 3 Bb5 or 3 Bc4. We will get to these other two moves in later games.

3...Nf6

Diagram 32. Position after 3...Nf6

Black develops his Knight toward the center attacking White's "e" Pawn. A symmetrical position is reached, and for a while, Black will be copying all of White's moves. Some of my students have told me that they become annoyed when their opponent copies their moves. In certain openings this may be acceptable to a point. However, if you are making sound moves, at some point Black cannot continue to copy your moves without making a mistake.

4 Bb5

White develops his Bishop actively by attacking Black's Knight. This indirectly puts pressure on Black's "e" Pawn, since the Knight on "c6" defends it.

4...Bb4

Black also develops his Bishop actively attacking White's Knight. This indirectly puts pressure on White's "e" Pawn, since the Knight on "c3" defends it.

He responds to the pressure on his "e" Pawn by putting similar pressure on White's "e" Pawn. A very aggressive and reasonable alternative would have been 4...Nd4, posting the Knight actively and attacking White's Bishop on "b5". Here 5 Nxe5 wouldn't win a Pawn because of 5...Qe7 6 Nf3 Nxb5 7 Nxb5 Qxe4+.

5 0-0

White gets his King out of the center and into safety. If White tried winning a Pawn with 5 Bxc6 dxc6 6 Nxe5, then Black could have recovered it easily after 6...Qe7.

5...0-0

Black also gets his King out of the center and into safety.

6 d3

This move frees the Bishop on "c1" and defends the White's "e" Pawn. Because Black would have no counterattack on White's "e" Pawn, White is threatening to win a Pawn with 7 Bxc6 followed by 8 Nxe5.

6...d6

Black defends his "e" Pawn while also freeing his Bishop on "c8".

7 Bg5

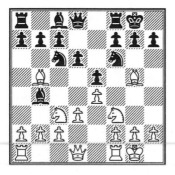

Diagram 33. Position after 7 Bg5

This move develops White's last minor piece while pinning Black's Knight on "f6". White now threatens to post his Knight on "d5" attacking Black's Bishop on "b4" and Black's pinned Knight on "f6".

7...Bxc3

White's Knight threatened to go to the strong outpost on "d5", so Black exchanges his Bishop for it. Though this gives White Doubled Pawns he will have compensation by having the Bishop pair, an open "b" file and a slightly stronger center when he captures toward the middle.

It would have been bad for Black to continue to copy White's moves with 7...Bg4. After 8 Bxf6 Bxf3 (8...Qxf6 would be meet by 9 Nd5 Qd8 10 Bxc6 bxc6 11 Nxb4) 9 Qxf3 Qxf6 10 Qxf6 gxf6 11 Nd5 White has a nice advantage.

After 7...Bg4 8 Bxf6, Black would do best to play 8...gxf6. However, after 9 Bxc6 bxc6 10 h3 Be6 11 Nh4 Black's Bishop pair would not give him enough compensation for his weakened Kingside and two sets of Doubled Pawns.

8 bxc3

White recovers his piece and brings his Pawn to a square that attacks the center.

8...Ne7

This is an interesting idea! Most books don't give a proper assessment of this move. There are two good reasons for it: First of all, Black plans to transfer his Knight to the Kingside while still covering important center squares; Secondly, Black can move his Pawn to "c6" attacking White's Bishop and supporting the future placement of a Pawn on "d5".

The most common move played here is 8...Qe7, which will prepare to connect Black's Rooks and open up "d8" for his Knight. The game might continue with 9 Re1 Nd8 10 d4 Ne6 11 Bc1 c5 with even chances. White dare not try to win a Pawn with 12 dxe5 dxe5 13 Nxe5??, because of 13...Nc7, and White has two pieces hanging!

9 Nh4

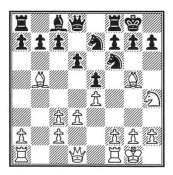

Diagram 34. Position after 9 Nh4

As a general rule *"Placing a Knight on the edge of the board is not good."* However, this move has some good advantages in this case; it allows White to open his "f" file

later on by moving a Pawn to "f4", gives his Queen access to the Kingside along the "d1-h5" diagonal, later the "f5" square may prove to be a good square to post the Knight on, and if Black plays 9...Ng6 White can double Black's Pawns after 10 Nxg6.

Doubling Black's Pawns with 9 Bxf6 is not as good as it looks. After 9...gxf6 White must contend with two Black possibilities: First, Black has the possibility of undoubling his Pawns by attacking in the center with 10...f5; Secondly, Black has the plan of attacking Black's Bishop with 10...c6 followed by attacking in the center with 11...d5.

9...c6

Black drives White's Bishop back and prepares to support an attack in the center with his "d" Pawn. This also opens the "d8-a5" diagonal, which may prove useful for the Queen later in the game.

10 Bc4

White removes his Bishop from the threat and places it along the more critical central "a2-g8" diagonal. However, playing 10 Ba4 would have been slightly better since it would prevent the Bishop from becoming a target for Black's "d" Pawn.

10...Be6?

Diagram 35. Position after 10...Be6

This will allow White to strip Black's King of his Pawn shield with a series of exchanges. See if you can find White's best move here without looking at the next move in the game.

Black missed his opportunity to take advantage of White's Bishop on "c4" by attacking it and gaining a great foothold on the center with 10...d5.

11 Bxf6

With this move White begins to strip away the Pawn shield which defends Black's castled King.

11...gxf6

This is Black's only move to recover his piece.

12 Bxe6

This removes another Pawn from shielding Black's castled King and makes the Pawn a target on "e6".

12...fxe6

Diagram 36. Position after 12...fxe6

Once again, Black had only one move to recover his piece.

13 Qg4+

White brings his Queen into play attacking both Black's King and the unprotected Pawn on "e6".

13...Kf7

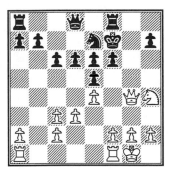

Diagram 37. Position after 13...Kf7

Black gets his King out of attack and defends his Pawn on "e6". It would have been much safer for Black's King to hide on "h8". However, after 13...Kh8 White wins a Pawn with 14 Qxe6 and also has the better position.

See if you can find White's best move here without looking at the next move in the game.

14 f4

This is a very important move for White. White plans to open up the "f" file for his Rook, taking advantage of Black's awkward King position.

14...Rg8?

Black is trying to get counterplay by attacking White's Queen and putting his Rook on an open file. However, this only drives White's Queen to another good attacking post and allows White to open up even more lines against Black's King.

Black's best defense here was 14...exf4. This would have avoided the brilliant sacrifice that White plays in the game. If Black played 14...Ng6 White gets a very strong attack with 15 f5.

15 Qh5+

White gets his Queen out of attack while attacking Black's King and unprotected "h" Pawn. White's Queen also now attacks "f7" which will prove crucial later in the game.

15...Kg7

This move gets the King out of attack while defending Black's threatened "h" Pawn.

16 fxe5

White opens up the "f" file for his Rook, which is consistent with his plan of opening up lines against Black's exposed King.

16...dxe5

Diagram 38. Position after 16...dxe5

Black recovers his Pawn with this move. Black would get checkmated quickly if he played 16...fxe5 17 Rf7+ Kh8 and now White can choose Black's method of execution with either 18 Rxh7++ or 18 Qxh7++.

See if you can find White's best move here without looking at the next move in the game.

17 Rxf6!

This is a nice sacrifice! It exposes Black's King to attack. The sacrifice will allow White to penetrate on the open "f" file. White is now threatening mate in two with 18 Rf7+ Kh8 19 Qxh7++.

17...Kxf6

Black accepts White's Rook sacrifice. Black's best chance is to accept and test the soundness of the sacrifice. Refusing the sacrifice will leave Black behind in material and White still has an attack.

If Black tried defending with 17...Ng6 then White wins easily after 18 Rxg6+! hxg6 19 Qxg6+ Kf8 20 Qh7!, and Black is defenseless against White's threat of 21 Rf1+.

18 Rf1+

White brings his Rook into play and attacks Black's King along the open "f" file.

18...Nf5

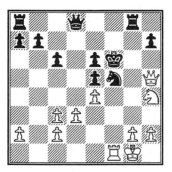

Diagram 39. Position after 18...Nf5

Black blocks White's attack on his King along the "f" file. If 18...Kg7 Black once again gets mated quickly after 19 Rf7+ Kh8 20 Qxh7++.

See if you can find White's best move here without looking at the next move in the book.

19 Nxf5!

This will allow White's rook to penetrate on the "f" file and is a very efficient way to win. The depth of thought behind this move will only become apparent at the end of the game. However, 19 exf5 would also have won easily after 19...Ke7 20 Qxh7+ Kd6 21 fxe6 and White has both a material advantage and an attack.

19...exf5

Black recovers the Knight and eliminates a piece that White would use in his attack against Black's King.

20 Rxf5 +

Diagram 40. Position after 20 Rxf5 +

This will allow White's Rook and Queen to work together in a coordinated attack against Black's King. White has achieved the goal mentioned earlier of penetrating the "f" file and gaining control of the important "f7" square.

20…Ke7

Black gets his King out of attack. Playing 20…Ke6 would transpose back into the game after 21 Qf7 +.

21 Qf7 +

White continues to attack Black's King and gives him no time to consolidate his position. This move puts the Queen on an ideal attacking post and will give White's Rook protection on "f6" when it continues its attack on Black's King.

21…Kd6

This is Black's only legal move to get his King out of check.

22 Rf6 +

The attack on the Black King continues. This move brings the Rook to the more active 6th rank and forces Black's King to either move further away from the protection of his pieces or lose his Queen.

22...Kc5

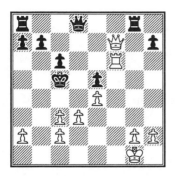

Diagram 41. Position after 22...Kc5

Black decides to take his chances with an exposed King rather than going into a lost endgame after 22...Qxf6 23 Qxf6+. White would win another Pawn and have a Queen and three Pawns against two Rooks.

Since White is a Rook down he cannot allow his attack to peter out against Black's King.

See if you can find White's best move here without looking at the next move in the book.

23 Qxb7

This seemingly quiet move is the only move that wins the game for White. White threatens several mates: 24 Qb4++, 24 Qxc6++ and 24 Rxc6++.

White would have nothing better than a draw by perpetual check after either 23 Qc4+ Kb6 24 Qb4+ Ka6 25 Qc4+ Ka5 26 Qb4+ Ka6, or 23 d4⼀ Kb6 24 Qb3⼀ Ka6 25 Qc4+ Kb6 26 Qb4+ Ka6.

23...Qb6

Diagram 42. Position after 23...Qb6

With this move Black's Queen prevents the threats of mate in one and challenges White's Queen. White needed to see his next move here in order for his 19th move to have been sound! This shows just how deep great players like Capablanca can think ahead.

See if you can find White's best move here without looking at the next move in the game.

24 Rxc6+!

White sacrifices his second Rook which will either win Black's Queen or mate Black's King.

24...Qxc6

Black chooses to allow mate rather than resigning or losing his Queen. After 24...Kb5 25 Rxb6+ axb6 White has a Queen and five Pawns against Black's two Rooks. At the master level it would be useless for Black to play on at that point.

25 Qb4++

Black's King is checkmated!

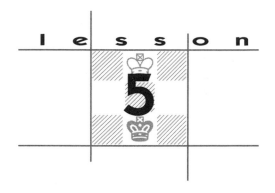

lesson

5

The Game That Made Me a Master

Snyder versus Gordon
Los Angeles, 1973

Opening: Two Knights Defense

The Western US Championship in 1973 gave me an opportunity to play against some really good players. At this time I had already achieved the rating of "Expert" and was hoping some day to make "Master". As a result of this last round game, I achieved a 5-0 score in the tournament, earned a Master's rating, became co-champion of the Western US and earned enough prize money to help me play in a fair number of other tournaments. This fifteen-move win against a Master will always be well remembered!

1 e4 e5 2 Nf3 Nc6 3 Bc4

Diagram 43. Position after 3 Bc4

Nowadays this is a less popular move than going into the Ruy Lopez with 3 Bb5. White develops his Bishop to the long "a2-g8" diagonal and attacks Black's weak point on "f7".

3...Nf6

This very active third move leads to the Two Knights Defense. Black develops his Knight toward the center attacking White's "e" Pawn.

4 d4

Diagram 44. Position after 4 d4

White boldly attacks in the center with a Pawn and frees his Bishop on "c1". This may lead to a variation known as the Max Lange Attack.

Another very common move for White here is to attack Black's "f" Pawn a second time with 4 Ng5. At this point Black will usually counterattack in the center with 4...d5, and play might continue 5 exd5 Na5 (better than 5...Nxd5 which allows White to get the advantage with either 6 d4 or 6 Nxf7, a sacrifice known as the "Fried Liver Attack") 6 Bb5+ c6 7 dxc6 bxc6 8 Be2 h6 9 Nf3 e4 10 Ne5 Bd6. This gambit gives Black active piece play for his Pawn.

4...Nxd4?

Diagram 45. Position after 4...Nxd4

This is an outright mistake. It will soon be shown how White has more than one way to take advantage of it. Black should have started to liquidate White's Pawn center with 4...exd4. From here the game might continue, 5 0-0 Nxe4 6 Re1 d5 7 Bxd5 Qxd5 8 Nc3 Qa5 9 Nxe4 Be6 10 Neg5 0-0-0 11 Nxe6 fxe6 12 Rxe6 Bd6 with an even game.

5 Nxd4

White recovers his Pawn and will get dominating control of the center with his pieces. Also good for White would have been 5 Bxf7+ Kxf7 6 Nxe5+ Kg8 7 Qxd4 c5 8 Qc4+ d5 9 exd5 Qxd5. Though Black is down a Pawn he has some compensation due to his Bishop pair and active pieces.

5...exd4

This is Black's only move to recover his Knight.

6 Qxd4

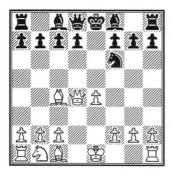

Diagram 46. Position after 6 Qxd4

This move recovers White's Pawn and brings the Queen to a dominating position in the center. As a general rule *"It isn't good to bring the Queen out early in the Opening."* However, there are many exceptions to this rule, and this is one of them. There is no effective way for Black to attack White's Queen in the center. White is now threatening to play 7 e5 and drive Black's Knight back to "g8".

6...d6

Black frees his bishop on "c8" and covers the important "e5" square.

7 Bg5

White develops his Bishop aggressively and pins Black's Knight. Developing White's Knight toward the center with 7 Nc3 would have also been good.

7...Be7

This move develops Black's Bishop, unpins his Knight and prepares to castle.

8 Nc3

This brings White's Knight toward the center and completes his minor piece development. It also gives White the option of castling Queenside.

8...0-0

Black gets his King out of the center and into relative safety by castling.

9 0-0-0

Diagram 47. Position after 9 0-0-0

White gets his King out of the center and brings his Rook to the half-open "d" file. As a general rule *"When both sides castle on opposite sides of the board this increases attacking chances."* This is because either side can advance the Pawns toward the enemy castled King without exposing his own King. Often in such games it becomes a race to see who can get to the other King first.

However, White has most of the attacking chances in this game due to his better control of the center.

9...Ne8

Black is trying to relieve the pressure on his somewhat cramped position by offering a Bishop exchange. However, this retreats his Knight to a less active square and will bring Black's Queen to a square where she is easily attacked.

A slightly better move for Black would have been to challenge White's active Bishop on "c4" with 9...Be6, though White would still have a very nice game after 10 e5 dxe5 11 Qxe5.

10 Bxe7

This brings Black's Queen to a square where she will become a target.

10...Qxe7

This is Black's only move to recover his Bishop.

11 Nd5

White brings his Knight to the active outpost on "d5" while gaining time by attacking Black's exposed Queen.

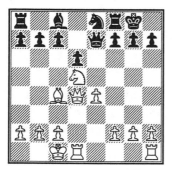

Diagram 48. Position after 11 Nd5

11...Qe5?

Black is trying to relieve pressure by offering an exchange of Queens. However, this will allow White to penetrate deep into his position and force the win of material.

Black's best move was to get his Queen out of attack with 11...Qd8. It might look funny for Black to have all of his pieces on his first rank, but sometimes you need to crawl on your belly when things get tough!

Black could not have won a Pawn after 11...Qg5+ 12 f4 Qxg2?. See if you can find White's best move here. If you found 13 Nxc7!, using the tactical motif known as an overworked defender, you were right! If Black plays 13...Nxc7, he would lose his Queen after 14 Rhg1. The Queen cannot move out of the way of the Rook because of 15 Qxg7++.

See if you can find White's best move here without looking at the next move in the game.

12 Qxe5

The exchange of Queens will open the "d" file to prepare for White's Rook to penetrate and removes Black's Queen as a defender of the critical "e7" square. You will soon see why this is important.

12...dxe5

This is Black's only move to recover his Queen.

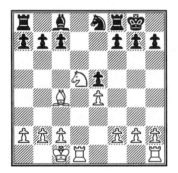

Diagram 49. Position after 12...dxe5

13 Ne7+

It was probably this move that Black overlooked. The Knight gets out of the way of White's Rook on the "d" file and attack's Black's Bishop on "c8". Because Black's King is in check this move also gains time for White's next move.

13...Kh8

This was Black's only legal move to get his King out of check.

14 Rd8

Diagram 50. Position after 14 Rd8

White has come right down the middle of the board with his Rook and Knight. Both of Black's minor pieces are pinned by White's Rook and the Bishop on "c8" is threatened. There is no way for Black to avoid the loss of material.

14...b5

This was desperation, hoping I would play either 15 Bxb5 or 15 Bxf7, which would be met by 15...Bb7, limiting his material loss.

15 Bd5

Black's problems are now compounded by the fact his Rook on "a8" is also attacked! At this point my kind opponent reached out his hand and resigned, congratulating me on my victory. I never expected to defeat my opponent in such a critical last round game in just 15 moves!

l e s s o n

6

Building Up a Kingside Attack

Hermann versus Charousek
Budapest, 1896

Opening: Two Knights Defense

Rudolph Charousek (1873–1900) was a Hungarian Master who learned the moves late in life, at the age of 16! He was soon to be recognized as one of the top players in the world. He placed first and second in several major tournaments despite ill health. He died of tuberculosis at the age of 26, when many of his competitors considered him to be a future World Champion.

The following game is considered to be one of Charousek's finest masterpieces. Black slowly builds up an attack on the Kingside. Then through the coordinated use of his Queen and two Bishops he secures a sparkling victory.

1 e4 e5 2 Nf3 Nc6 3 Bc4 Nf6 4 Nc3

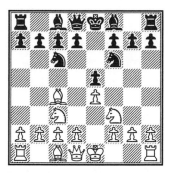

Diagram 51. Position after 4 Nc3

This normal-looking developing move, which develops a Knight toward the center, is not considered to be very strong here because of what my students call "The Knight sacrifice Pawn fork trick"!

4...Nxe4

Black temporarily sacrifices his Knight to set up a Pawn fork and eliminate White's one center Pawn. As a result Black will have a good foothold in the center and his Bishops will be freed for easy development.

5 Nxe4

White removes Black's active Knight on "e4". Black may lose his ability to castle after 5 Bxf7+ Kxf7 6 Nxe4 but he gets a strong Pawn center, active pieces and a safe King after 6...d5. The aggressive looking 7 Neg5+ Kg8 8 d4 or 8 d3 is simply met with 8...h6 driving White's Knight back to "h3".

5...d5

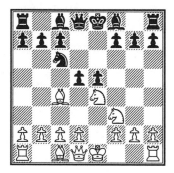

Diagram 52. Position after 5...d5

This move forks White's Bishop and Knight and frees the Bishop on "c8".

6 Bxd5?

White must return the minor piece and therefore he decides to immediately get a Pawn for his Bishop. However, this will not allow White to fight for the center by getting a Pawn to "d4". White would have done better to play 6 Bd3 dxe4 7 Bxe4 Bd6 8 d4 with an equal game.

6...Qxd5

Black recovers his piece and threatens White's Knight on "e4".

7 Nc3

White gets his Knight out of attack while attacking Black's Queen. A reasonable looking move for White would have been to defend the Knight and free the Bishop on "c1" with 7 d3. However, after Black pins the Knight with 7...Bg4 he has better control of the center and more active pieces.

7...Qd8

Diagram 53. Position after 7...Qd8

Many players would have a difficult time deciding where to place their attacked Queen. For a great master like Charousek this decision was easy. He knew that his Queen should not block the development of his Bishops and that his best chances were on the Kingside. The Queen on "d8" can easily aid in an attack on the Kingside by either going to "f6" or "h4", or as in the game to "e8" followed by either going to "g6" or "h5". Black has in mind a long-term plan with numerous options for his Queen.

8 0-0

White gets his King out of the center and into safety while planning to shift his Rook to the half-open "e" file.

8...Bd6

This move develops a Bishop, prepares to castle and gives extra protection to the "e" Pawn. Since White's Rook can be used to attack along the "e" file, the "e" Pawn will soon be under attack twice. Note that later in the game the Bishop will come into play in Black's Kingside attack on the "b8-h2" diagonal. Once again, long term planning is the key to success when playing chess!

9 d3

White frees his Bishop on "c1" and covers the important "e4" square. Do you see what would happen if White played more aggressively with 9 d4? After 9...Nxd4 10 Nxd4 exd4 White could not recover his Pawn with 11 Qxd4 because of the discovered attack after 11...Bxh2+ 12 Kxh2 Qxd4.

9...0-0

Black gets his King out of the center and into safety while bringing his Rook to the "f" file. Black's Rook on "f8" will back up Black's "f" Pawn when it is advanced as part of Black's plan to attack on the Kingside. Another reasonable move would have been to develop actively and pin White's Knight with 9...Bg4.

10 h3

Diagram 54. Position after 10 h3

White prevents his Knight from being pinned with 10...Bg4. The drawback is that White weakens his Kingside Pawn structure. The "h" Pawn may become a target later on.

10...f5

This is Black's first obvious indication that he may have a Kingside attack in mind! The advance of the "f" Pawn may support a Kingside attack in the following possible ways:

1. the "e" or "f" Pawn is now protected by another Pawn when advanced,
2. Black's Rook on "f8" may back up the advance of the "f" Pawn or may be brought into play by going to "f6" and then "g6", and
3. the "e8-h5" diagonal is opened for possible use by Black's Queen after it goes to "e8"— she may then attack from "g6" or "h5".

11 Re1

White brings his rook onto the half-open file and ties down Black's pieces to the defense of his "e" Pawn. White does best at this point to play actively.

11...Bd7?

Black develops his Bishop while connecting his Rooks. This however should have given White a chance to slow down Black's attack. The correct way for Black to proceed would have been with 11...Qf6. If Black had played 12 Bg5, Black's Queen would have been able to go to the natural attacking post on "g6".

12 Qe2?

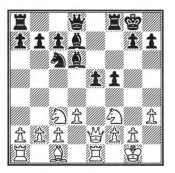

Diagram 55. Position after 12 Qe2

White places his Queen on a square where she easily becomes a target. Instead White should have played 12 Bg5 driving Black's Queen to a less active square after 12...Qc8. If Black then decided to try and shift his Queen toward the Kingside with 12...Qe8, then White could have played 13 Bf4!, tying Black's pieces down to the defense of his "e" Pawn.

12...Qe8

Black brings his Queen to the "e8-h5" diagonal where she can assist in the Kingside build-up by going to "g6" or "h5". However, Black had a couple of very good alternatives such as 12...Nd4, taking the strong outpost and attacking White's Queen. Then if White played 13 Nxd4, Black would open his "e" file exposing White's Queen to a future attack after 13...exd4. The other good alternative would have been for Black to bring his Queen into play on the Kingside with 12...Qf6.

13 Be3

White develops his Bishop to its most active available post. However, the Bishop is a target on "e3" to Black's "f" Pawn. It would have been a better idea for White to try and relieve the pressure by seeking exchanges and attacking Black's potentially strong Bishop on "d6" with 13 Nb5.

13...Qg6

Diagram 56. Position after 13...Qg6

The Queen is brought into play to assist in the Kingside attack. She is aiming directly at White's King and Black now threatens 14...f4 15 Bd2 Bxh3.

14 Kh1

White unpins his "g" Pawn so that his "h" Pawn will be defended against Black's threat.

14...f4

Black drives back White's Bishop on "e3" while opening the diagonal for Black's Bishop on "d7" to join the attack on the Kingside.

15 Bd2

Since the Bishop was threatened White retreats it to the only square that keeps White's Rooks connected.

15...Nd4

Diagram 57. Position after 15...Nd4

Black posts his Knight actively on the natural "d4" outpost attacking White's exposed Queen on "e2". Black also challenges White's Knight on "f3" which is his important Kingside defender.

16 Nxd4?

The Knight on "f3" was blockading the critical advance of Black's "f" Pawn. Therefore, White's idea of making an even exchange to reduce Black's attack does not work well here.

A better move for White would have been to get his Queen out of attack while continuing to protect the Knight on "f3" with 16 Qd1. Black could have then continued his attack with 16...Qh6 which threatens both 17...Bg4 and 17...Bxh3.

16...exd4

Black recovers his Knight while attacking White's Knight on "c3" and opening up the "e" file. White's Queen is a possible target along the open "e" file.

17 Ne4

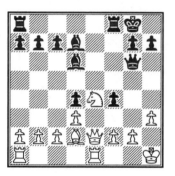

Diagram 58. Position after 17 Ne4

White gets his Knight out of attack while centralizing it and blocking the "e" file. See if you can find Black's best move here without looking at the next move in the game.

17...f3

This move attacks White's Queen, threatens mate on "g2" and will force the opening of lines against White's King.

18 gxf3

White eliminates Black's aggressive Pawn but the immediate opening of lines against White's King will prove to be quickly fatal. White could have held out longer by retreating his attacked Queen and defending against Black's mate threat on "g2" with 18 Qf1. However, after 18...fxg2+ 19 Qxg2 Qh5 White is in serious trouble.

18...Bxh3

Black recovers the Pawn, brings his Bishop into the attack and threatens 19...Qg2++.

19 Rg1

White defends against the mate threat on "g2" while trying to get as much counterplay as possible by attacking Black's Queen.

19...Qh5

Diagram 59. Position after 19...Qh5.

This move gets the Black Queen out of attack and aims her directly at White's King. Black is threatening 20...Bf1++!

20 Rg5

White opens up "g1" as a possible escape square for his King while attacking Black's Queen.

20...Qh4

Black gets his Queen out of attack with threats such as 21...Bg4+ 22 Kg1 Qh2+ Kf1 23 Qh1++ or 21...Bf1+.

21 Kg1

Diagram 60. Position after 21 Kg1

White gets his King off of the same file as Black's Queen, avoiding the discovered attack threats.

See if you can find Black's best move here without looking at the next move in the game.

21...Bh2+!

The poor White King is driven back onto the "h" file!

22 Kh1

White cannot accept Black's Bishop sacrifice. If White took the Bishop with 22 Kxh2, then Black wins White's Queen with a discovered check after 22...Bf1+.

22...Bf1

This is just one of numerous moves Black had that would win material. Black attacks White's Queen and sets up a discovered attack.

Another good move was 22...Bf4, attacking Black's Rook and setting up discovered check threats such as 23...Bg4+ 24 Kg1 Qh2+ 25 Kf1 Qh1++.

23 Qd1

Diagram 61. Position after 23 Qd1

White gets his Queen out of attack, but allows Black to win with a brilliant move. White could have lasted longer with 23 Rg4 Qh5 24 Rg5 Bxe2 25 Rxh5 Bxf3+ 26 Kxh2 Bxh5, but being down the exchange and a Pawn in the endgame didn't appeal to White.

See if you can find Black's best move here without looking at the next move in the game.

23...Be2!

This move is awesome! It threatens White's Queen and prevents White's King from escaping to "e2". White would get checkmated quickly if he captures the Bishop after 24 Qxe2 Bg3+ 25 Kg1 Qh2+ 26 Kf1 Qh1++. White resigned here.

l e s s o n

7

Understanding the Opening

Snyder versus Arnold
Chicago, 1973

Opening: Giuoco Piano

It does little good to be well prepared for middlegame and endgame strategy if you don't survive the opening. I teach a well-rounded and sound opening system to all of my students. It is difficult to predict what type of tactics and endgame positions you will need to know before the start of a game. However, if you have a thorough knowledge of the opening, it will come in handy in every game you play.

1 e4 e5 2 Nf3 Nc6 3 Bc4 Bc5

Diagram 62. Position after 3...Bc5

This is a good alternative to playing 3...Nf6. Black develops his Bishop to the active "g1-a7" diagonal.

4 d3

This is often considered to be a conservative way of playing the Giuoco Piano. However, many times it can lead to an active game with lots of tactics. White frees his Bishop on "c1" and defends his Pawn on "e4" and Bishop on "c4".

A more active move here would have been 4 c3 preparing to support White's Pawn advance to "d4". The main opening line might continue, 4...Nf6 5 d4 exd4 6 cxd4 Bb4+ 7 Nc3 (or 7 Bd2 Bxd2+ 8 Nbxd2 d5 9 exd5 Nxd5 10 Qb3 Nce7 11 0-0 0-0 12 Rfe1 c6 and White has an isolated "d" Pawn but active piece play as compensation) Nxe4 8 0-0 Bxc3 9 d5 (if 9 bxc3 then 9...d5 is good for Black, not 9...Nxc3?? because of 10 Qe1+ forking King and Knight) Bf6 10 Re1 Ne7 11 Rxe4 d6 12 Bg5 Bxg5 13 Nxg5 h6 14 Qe2 hxg5 15 Re1 Be6 16 dxe6 f6 17 Re3 c6 18 Rh3 Rxh3 19 gxh3 g6 and White has very little to show for the Pawn he lost.

Another well-known opening here is the Evan's Gambit. White offers a Pawn sacrifice with 4 b4 which might continue, 4...Bxb4 5 c3 Ba5 6 d4 d6 7 Qb3 Qd7 9 dxe5 Bb6 10 exd6 (Black also gets a good game after 10 Bb5 a6) Na5 11 Qb4 Nxc4 12 Qxc4 Qxd6 and Black's better Pawn structure and Bishop pair give him a slight advantage.

4...Nf6

Black develops his Knight actively toward the center.

5 Nc3

White also develops his Knight actively toward the center.

5...d6

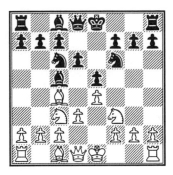

Diagram 63. Position after 5...d6

Black frees his Bishop on "c8" and defends his Pawn on "e5" and Bishop on "c5". A symmetrical position has been reached and White has a couple of alternatives here.

6 Be3

White develops his Bishop toward the center and challenges Black's active Bishop on "c5". The other alternative was to develop the Bishop to "g5" and pin Black's Knight. However, after 6 Bg5 Black can easily equalize with 6...Na5, resulting in an exchange of Black's Knight for White's good Bishop.

6...0-0

Black gets his King out of the center, but in this instance it is risky to commit the King to being on the Kingside so early. A good alternative would have been to play 6...Bb6. This would allow 7 Bxb6 to be met by 7...axb6, capturing toward the center and creating an open file for the Rook on "a8". Therefore, after 6...Bb6 White would do better to play 7 Qd2 preparing for possible Queenside castling with about even chances.

Black chooses not to double White's Pawns with 6...Bxe3 because White would then capture toward the center and open his "f" file with 7 fxe3.

7 Bg5

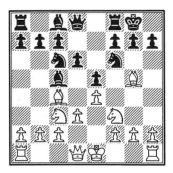

Diagram 64. Position after 7 Bg5

As a general rule *"You don't want to move the same piece twice in the opening."* However, in this case, Black's King is now on the Kingside and pinning the Knight on "f6" is much stronger. Therefore, White doesn't mind moving his Bishop twice in a row. White's plan now is to pile up on Black's pinned Knight on "f6" with 8 Nd5. White will then try to weaken Black's castled position by capturing on "f6".

7...Be6

Black develops his Bishop toward the center and challenges White's active Bishop on "c4". Black also plans to counter White's plan by exchanging his Bishop for White's soon to be strongly posted Knight on "d5".

8 Nd5

Diagram 65. Position after 8 Nd5

White follows through with his plan. He posts his Knight strongly on the "d5" outpost and piles up on Black's pinned Knight on "f6".

8...Bxd5

This removes White's actively posted Knight on "d5". Black had to concern himself with White's threat of capturing on "f6" and exposing Black's King.

9 Bxd5

White recovers his piece. White didn't want to recover the piece with 9 exd5 because his Bishop on "c4" would be blocked and he would have had doubled Pawns.

9...Qe7?

Black's Queen will become a target on "e7". Black's idea is to connect his Rooks and bring his Queen to a more active square. However, if Black drives White's Bishop back with 9...h6 10 Bxc6 bxc6 11 Bh4 g5 12 Bg3 then Black's Kingside has been severely weakened.

10 Nh4!

Diagram 66. Position after 10 Nh4

There are three reasons behind this move:

1. White's Knight has the possibility of entering the very strong post on "f5" which would also attack Black's Queen,
2. it opens up the "d1-h5" diagonal for White's Queen to be able to attack on the Kingside, and
3. it allows for the possibility of White moving his Pawn to "f4", which may allow for the Rook to be used on the "f" file.

10...g6?

Black prevents White's Knight from going to "f5". However, this move greatly weakens the dark squares around Black's castled King.

It would have been better to allow the entry of Black's Knight and play 10...h6 11 Nf5 Qd8 12 Bh4. White's Bishop pair and more actively placed pieces give him the advantage.

11 Bxc6

Here White had several alternatives that would give him a nice advantage. White's idea is to pile up on the pinned Knight on "f6" and to provoke Black to weaken his Kingside further. The move in the game removes Black's potentially active Knight from possibly entering "d4" when White's Queen gets to "f3".

However, even if White had played 11Qf3 right away, White still would get the advantage after 11...Nd4 12 Qxf6 Qxf6 13 Bxf6 Nxc2+ 14 Ke2 Nxa1 15 Rxa1 c6 16 Bb3. Here White has two minor pieces for a Rook and Pawn. White's excellently placed Bishops greatly restrict Black's activity. Another possibility for White would have been to play 11 c3, preventing Black's Knight from entering "d4".

11...bxc6

This is the only move that recovers the minor piece.

12 Qf3

Diagram 67. Position after 10 Qf3

White continues with his plan of attacking Black's Knight on "f6" with a second piece and provoking Black to weaken himself on the Kingside.

12...Kg7

Since Black's Knight is attacked a second time, it is defended by a second piece to avoid losing it. As a general rule *"All being equal, if a piece is defended by the same number of pieces that are attacking it, it is sufficiently protected."*

13 Qh3

White is setting up a couple of threats involving the Queen's potential ability to attack the "h6" square. This should provoke Black to weaken his Kingside Pawn shield to defend against the threats. One of the threats is to play 14 Bh6+ winning the exchange after 14...Kg8 15 Bxf8. If 14...Kxh6 then, 15 Nf5+ Kg5 16 Qh4++.

13...Rfe8?

Diagram 68. Position after 13...Rfe8

Black saw White's threat of 14 Bh6+ and responded to it by moving his Rook from "f8". However, Black overlooked White's even bigger threat! Black's best chance was to go ahead and weaken his castled King's Pawn shield with 13...h5.

See if you can find White's best move here without looking at the next move in the game.

14 Nf5+!

This is a clearance sacrifice to allow for the penetration of White's Queen to "h6".

14...gxf5

Because White's Knight is forking the King and Queen Black has little choice but to accept the sacrifice.

15 Qh6+

White's Queen penetrates, attacking Black's Knight on "f6" a second time and resulting in the win of Black's Queen. Black has nothing better than 15...Kg8 16 Bxf6 Qxf6 (if 16...Qf8 then 17 Qg5+ Qg7 18 Qxg7++) 17 Qxf6. Since Black must lose his Queen, he resigned here.

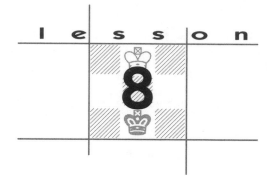

l e s s o n

8

Taking Advantage
of an Unsound Sacrifice

Baer (Switzerland) versus Snyder (USA)
International Correspondence Master Class
Tournament, 1977–1978

Opening: Ruy Lopez

White sacrifices a Rook for a Knight and Pawn leading to a complicated middlegame. Black holds onto his material advantage and heads for the endgame.

1 e4 e5 2 Nf3 Nc6 3 Bb5

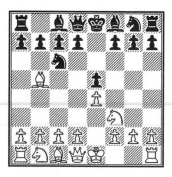

Diagram 69. Position after 3 Bb5

This move initiates one of the strongest and most popular openings, the Ruy Lopez. I often joke with my students that the Bishop attacks the Knight (on "c6"), which defends the Pawn (on "e5"), which is under attack by the Knight (on "f3"), which lives in the house that Jack built. In other words the Pawn on "e5" is indirectly having pressure placed on it. Black must be on guard against the possibility of White exchanging his Bishop for Black's Knight on "c6", which would remove the protection of Black's "e" Pawn.

3...Bc5

This is known as the "Classical Variation" of the Ruy Lopez. Black develops his Bishop to the long and active "g1-a7" diagonal. The major drawback is that the Bishop on "c5" is attacked if White gets a Pawn to "d4".

4 c3

Diagram 70. Position after 4 c3

White prepares to support the placement of a Pawn on "d4". Also playable, but less active, would have been 4 0-0.

4...f5

Black offers his "f" Pawn as a gambit. A gambit is the sacrifice of a Pawn or a piece in the opening with the hope of obtaining a good position in return for it. By giving up his "f" Pawn, Black will remove a White Pawn from the center and make it a potential target for the Bishop on the "c8-h3" diagonal, and, after castling for a Rook on the half-open "f" file.

The most common move here for Black is to develop his Knight toward the center and prepare for castling with 4...Nf6. However, White gets a good game after 5 0-0 0-0 6 d4.

5 exf5

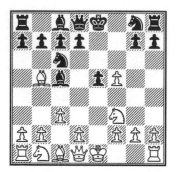

Diagram 71. Position after 5 exf5

White accepts Black's gambited Pawn. Many years ago, I used this opening line as Black extensively in tournaments and correspondence play.

It is much stronger for White to immediately attack in the center with 5d4. My game against Stern of Germany continued, 5...fxe4 6 Bxc6 dxc6 7 Nfd2 Bd6 8 dxe5 e3 (8...Bxe5?? would lose a Bishop due to a Queen fork after 9 Qh5+) 9 exd6! (this is a major improvement on the old book move, 9 fxe3, which may continue, 9...Bc5 10 Qh5+ g6 11 Qf3 Qh4+ 12 g3 Qh3 and Black is holding his own) exd2+ 10 Nxd2 Qxd6 11 0-0 Be6 12 Qh5+ g6 13 Qg5. Here Black is paralyzed, as he cannot castle Queenside and his Knight cannot be developed to "f6".

As a result of White's innovation on move 9 above, I gave up playing this line. Part of a serious player's training is to be able to recognize when an opening line is not good, and to be flexible enough to accept change!

5...e4

Black plays aggressively attempting to gain more space in the center and attacking White's Knight on "f3".

6 d4

White doesn't have a good square for his threatened Knight. Therefore, White counter-attacks in the center while threatening Black's Bishop on "c5" and creating a possible post on "e5" for his Knight.

6...exf3

Black trades off his Bishop for White's potentially strong Knight and plans to break up White's Kingside Pawns. White will have two sets of doubled Pawns, which are potential targets for Black.

7 dxc5

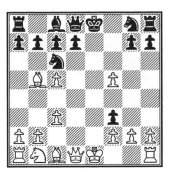

Diagram 72. Position after 7 dxc5

White recovers his minor piece.

7...Qe7+

Black first takes command of the "e" file with his Queen before capturing on "g2". When Black captures on "g2" he releases control of the "e2" square, which would allow White to place his Queen there. White's Bishop will also be pinned when it goes to "e3".

If Black had played 7...fxg2, then White could have played 8 Qh5+ g6 9 Qe2+ with an excellent position due to his active pieces.

8 Be3

White gets his King out of check while developing his Bishop.

8...fxg2

This gives White three isolated Pawns on the Kingside while getting the threatened Pawn out of attack on a temporary basis. However, Black's Pawn on "g2" will have no hope of survival. White will be able to win the Pawn and get play along the "g" file.

9 Rg1

White gets his Rook out of attack while attacking White's weak "g" Pawn.

9...Nf6

Black develops his Knight toward the center and prepares to castle.

10 Qf3

Diagram 73. Position after 10 Qf3

White's Queen is planning to capture Black's "g" Pawn to apply strong pressure along the "g" file. The Queen temporarily defends the weak Pawn on "f5" while getting off the "d1" square to clear the way for Queenside castling.

10...0-0

Black gets his King out of the center while bringing his Rook onto the half open "f" file. This will also make it easier for Black to win the Pawn on "f5".

11 Nd2

This move completes White's minor piece development and makes castling on the Queenside possible. White is in no rush to capture Black's weak Pawn on "g2". It isn't going anywhere except off the board!

11...d6

Black frees his Bishop on "c8" and begins to put pressure on White's weak Pawn on "f5". It is true that this will allow White to trade off his weak Pawn on "c5". However, freeing the Bishop on "c8" is more important.

12 0-0-0

White gets his King out of the center while bringing his Rook into play on the half-open "d" file. It would have been risky for White to go Pawn grabbing with 12 Bxc6 bxc6 13 Qxc6 Bxf5. Black's open lines and active pieces would put White's King in an uncomfortable situation.

12...Ne5

Black forces the issue. He gets his Knight out of attack while actively posting it in the center and attacking White's Queen.

13 Qxg2

White gets his Queen out of attack while finally winning Black's weak "g" Pawn and putting pressure along the half-open "g" file. Black's Queen is tied down to the defense of the Pawn on "g7". White had little choice himself but to give up his weak "f" Pawn.

13...Bxf5

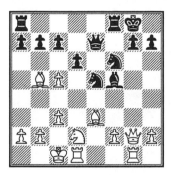

Diagram 74. Position after 13...Bxf5

This wins White's weak "f" Pawn, develops Black's Bishop to the long open "b1-h7" diagonal and connects his Rooks.

14 Nc4?

White brings his Knight actively into play attacking Black's Pawn on "d6" a third time and challenging Black's centralized Knight. However, White must give up a Rook for a Knight and Pawn. Unfortunately for White, he doesn't get enough for his sacrifice.

It would have been better for White to play either 14 f4 Ng6, or 14 Rde1 a6 15 Be2 Qd7 with about even chances in both cases. See if you can find Black's best move here without looking at the next move in the game.

14...Nd3+

This attack on White's King will force him to sacrifice material.

15 Rxd3

White has little choice but to give up his Rook for Black's Knight. Otherwise, after 15 Kd2 Black can win the "c" Pawn and open up the "d" file against White's exposed King with 15...dxc5. White would lose his Queen after 15 Kc2?? or Kb1?? to 15...Ne1+.

15...Bxd3

This captures a Rook, leaving Black with a material advantage.

16 cxd6

This is one of a variety of ways that White could get a Pawn after sacrificing the exchange. A player is said to *"lose the exchange"* when he/she has lost a Rook for a minor piece (a Knight or Bishop). A player is said to *"win the exchange"* when he/she has won a Rook for a minor piece.

A slightly better way to win the Pawn would have been to play 16 Nxd6 with a discovered attack on Black's Bishop on "d3". However, Black would still have come out on top after 16...Bxb5 17 Nxb5 Qd7.

16...cxd6

Black removes White's menacing Pawn.

17 Nxd6

Diagram 75. Position after 17 Nxd6

White wins Black's Pawn due to the discovered attack on Black's Bishop on "d3". White could not win Black's Knight with 17...Qxd6 because of 18 Qxg7++.

17...Bg6

Black gets his Bishop out of attack while blocking White's pressure along the "g" file and threatening 18...Qxd6. However, a better alternative for Black would have been to simplify and trade off the Bishops with 17...Bxb5 18 Nxb5 Rf7.

18 Bc4+

White repositions his Bishop on the long "a2-g8" diagonal while attacking Black's King. However, there was no rush for this and simply defending the Knight with the more subtle 18 Bc5 would have been better.

18...Kh8

This is the only way for Black to get his King out of attack without losing material. Black is now threatening to win White's Knight with 19...Qxd6.

19 Bc5

Diagram 76. Position after 19 Bc5

White defends the Knight on "d6" and threatens 20 Nf7+, with a discovered attack on Black's Queen.

19...Qe5

Black takes care of White's threat of 20 Nf7+ by getting the Queen off of the same diagonal as White's Bishop. Black's Queen is actively centralized and threatens White's Bishop on "c5" as well as 20 Qf4+. White must also concern himself with the future possibility of Black getting his Queen along the "b1-h7" diagonal. However, 19...Qc7 would have also been good for Black.

20 Qg5

White has little choice but to challenge Black's actively posted Queen to prevent her threats from becoming an execution!

20...Nd7

This move defends Black's Queen, threatens White's Bishop on "c5" and opens up an attack on White's "f" Pawn by the Rook of "f8". Black wants to trade Queens on his terms. If Black played 20...Qxg5, White would bring his Rook into play with 21 Rxg5.

Black could have gone Pawn grabbing with 20...Qxh2. However, Black wanted to simplify the game since he already had a material advantage and didn't want to allow White to obtain counterplay by attacking the pinned Bishop on "g6" with 21 Bd3.

21 Qxe5

Exchanging Queens was the only good way of taking care of Black's threat on White's Bishop on "c5".

21...Nxe5

Diagram 77. Position after 21...Nxe5

Black recovers the Queen and posts his Knight actively in the center while attacking White's Bishop on "c4". Black's advantages here consist of having a Rook against a Bishop and Pawn, and the better Pawn structure due to White's Kingside Pawns being isolated. Black's plan here is to drive White's pieces to less active squares while bringing his own pieces to more active squares. This will neutralize the effectiveness of White's aggressively posted pieces.

22 Be2

White wants to preserve his Bishop pair and therefore he removes it from being under attack by Black's Knight. On "e2" the Bishop maintains the flexibility of covering both sides of the board and is not an easy target for Black's pieces.

22...b6

This removes the pressure of White's pieces attacking Black's Queenside Pawns while attacking and driving back White's actively posted Bishop on "c5".

23 Bd4

White gets his Bishop out of attack by the Pawn on "b6" while attacking and driving away Black's Knight from its center post.

23...Nc6

Black gets his Knight out of attack while attacking White's actively posted Bishop on "d4". Black threatens to win White's "f" Pawn with 24...Nxd4 25 cxd4 Rxf2.

24 Be3

This is the only square available to White's Bishop to get it out of attack by Black's pieces.

24...Rad8

Diagram 78. Position after 24...Rad8

Black brings his last piece into play and threatens White's last aggressively posted piece. Black is accomplishing his goal of driving White's pieces to less active squares while bringing his pieces to more active squares. Just notice the difference in the position from three moves ago!

25 Rd1

Now that the "g" file is not an effective file for the Rook, White brings his Rook to a more important center file and defends his last actively posted piece.

25...Rf6

This forces the issue. Black threatens White's actively posted Knight, which must now retreat.

26 Nc4

White had no choice but to retreat his Knight or lose it. White chooses a square for the Knight which is close to the center to keep it as active as possible. This also opens up White's Rook on the "d" file challenging Black's Rook.

26...Rxd1 +

Black didn't want White to play 27 Rxd8+ which would require his Knight to retreat to a less active square after 27...Nxd8. Therefore, Black decided to exchange Rooks using the principle of making even exchanges of pieces when ahead in material.

27 Bxd1?

Diagram 79. Position after 27 Bxd1

White recaptures with the wrong piece. Although there is little difference in White's King being on "c1" or "d1", the Bishop is more actively placed on "e2" than "d1".

27...Bf7

Black repositions his Bishop to apply pressure to White's unprotected Knight and Pawn along the "a2-g8" diagonal. This will require White to tie down a piece to the defense of his Knight or to retreat it again.

28 Bb3

The Bishop would be more flexibly located on "e2". White defends his Knight while trying to challenge Black's Bishop along the "a2-g8" diagonal. However, this only sets up another exchange, which favors Black.

White could have also considered retreating his Knight with 28 Nd2 planning to meet 28...Bxa2? with 29 b3 trapping Black's Bishop. However, it is understandable that, with all the retreating White has recently done, he wanted to make a more active move.

28...Kg8

Black begins to bring his King into play. As a general rule *"The King should be used as an active fighting piece in the endgame."*

29 Nd2?

Since even exchanges of pieces favor Black who is ahead in material, White would have done better to bring his King to a more active location with 29 Kc2.

29...Bxb3

Black exchanges down to a more simplified endgame, which makes it easier to utilize his material advantage. Black is clearly winning at this point. White now has the uncomfortable choice of either doubling his Pawns or putting his Knight on a less active square.

30 axb3

Diagram 80. Position after 30 axb3

White chooses to recover his piece and accept doubled Pawns instead of putting his Knight on a less active square.

30...Rf5

Black's plan is to attack White's weak isolated Pawns on the Kingside using both his Rook and Knight. If White loses his "h" Pawn then Black will have an outside passed "h" Pawn, making victory very easy.

This move prepares to possibly attack White's weak "h" Pawn by bringing the Rook to "h5". It will also prevent White from pinning the Knight to the Rook with Bd4 when the Knight goes to "e5". However, it would have also been good for Black to play 30...Ne5 31 Bd4 Rf5.

31 Kc2

This move brings the King to a slightly more active square. However, it would have been better for White to play 32 Kd1 with the idea of bringing his King toward the defense of his weak Kingside Pawns.

31...Ne5

Black's Knight is centralized and is heading toward the Kingside to attack White's weak Pawns there.

32 Ne4

White centralizes his Knight and hopes to use it actively to get some counterplay.

32...Ng4

This brings the Knight into play on the Kingside, attacking White's two isolated Pawns and the Bishop on "e3". White cannot avoid the loss of his "h" Pawn at this point.

Diagram 81. Position after 32...Ng4

33 Bd4

This move is a waste of time. White shouldn't have bothered worrying about Black trading his Knight for White's Bishop on "e3" since the Knight was going after the "h" Pawn. White's best chance for counterplay would have been to activate his King further with 33 Kd3 and after 33...Nxh2 to get a passed Pawn with moves like 34 c4 followed by 35 b4 and 36 c5.

33...Nxh2

Black wins White's "h" Pawn, creating an outside passed Pawn.

34 Nd6

White realizes that playing conservatively will make Black's victory easy after he begins to advance his Kingside Pawns. Therefore, White does his best to try to obtain as much counterplay as possible by using his Knight aggressively.

34...Rd5

Black gets his Rook out of attack while placing it on an active central post and attacking White's Knight.

35 Nc8

White gets his Knight out of attack and threatens Black's "a" Pawn.

35...Rd7

Diagram 82. Position after 35...Rd7

Black defends the "a" Pawn and traps White's Knight.

36 Nxa7

This is pure desperation. Black's plan of moving his Knight to "f3" followed by advancing his passed "h" Pawn and moving his King toward White's trapped Knight was just too much for White to handle! White hopes to eliminate Black's Queenside Pawns to obtain three connected passed Pawns. However, this plan is far too slow to hope for success.

36...Rxa7

Black wins White's Knight.

37 Bxb6

White removes Black's last Queenside Pawn.

37...Rb7

Black gets his Rook out of attack while gaining time by attacking White's Bishop.

38 Be3

White gets his Bishop out of attack. Black's next move will clarify matters and show White the hopelessness of his situation. See if you can find Black's best move here without looking at the next move in the game.

Diagram 83. Position after 38 Be3

38...h5

White realizes that Black's outside Passed "h" Pawn will easily bring home victory and that there is no time to advance the Queenside Pawns. Being a Rook down, White resigned here.

l e s s o n

9

Sacrificing a Pawn
for Long Term Pressure

Ken Rogoff versus Sammy Reshevsky
US Championship, 1974

Opening: Ruy Lopez

Sammy Reshevsky (1911–1992) learned to play chess at the age of four. By the time he was eight he was considered to be a chess prodigy and was giving simultaneous exhibitions across Europe and the United States. Reshevsky won the US Championship numerous times and had an even score in an aborted match against Bobby Fischer in 1961.

Black sacrifices a Pawn early in the game and obtains strong pressure along open files. He keeps his opponent tied down while building up for a well-timed breakthrough.

1 e4 e5 2 Nf3 Nc6 3 Bb5 a6

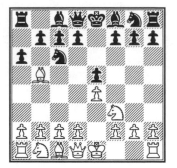

Diagram 84. Position after 3…a6

This is the most common third move for Black in the Ruy Lopez. Black forces White's Bishop either to retreat or to be exchanged for the Knight on "c6". If White retreats his Bishop to "a4" then Black will have the option, at a time of his choosing, to drive the Bishop even further back by moving a Pawn to "b5". As mentioned before I often jokingly say to my students about this move, "Black attacks the Bishop, which attacks the Knight, which defends the Pawn, that is under attack by the Knight that lives in the house that Jack built".

4 Bxc6

White exchanges his Bishop for Black's Knight, giving up the Bishop pair in order to double Black's Pawns. This also removes an important defender of the Pawn on "e5". When 4 Bxc6 is played, it is known as the "Exchange Variation" of the Ruy Lopez.

4…dxc6

Diagram 85. Position after 4…dxc6

Black recovers his minor piece while freeing his Bishop on the "c8-h3" diagonal and Queen on the "d1-d8" file. In this case freeing his pieces is more important than following the general rule, *"You should capture toward the center with Pawns in the Opening."*

5 0-0

White removes his King from the center and activates his Rook. White could not have won a Pawn with 5 Nxe5 because of 5…Qd4 6 Nf3 Qxe4+ 7 Qe2 Qxe2+ 8 Kxe2 and Black's Bishop pair and ability to castle Queenside more than compensate for his doubled Pawns.

White now threatens to win a Pawn with 6 Nxe5. This is because the same idea to recover the Pawn by playing 6…Qd4 7 Nf3 Qxe4?? is met by 8 Re1, pinning and winning Black's Queen.

5…Qd6

Diagram 86. Position after 5…Qd6

Black defends the "e" Pawn and begins to clear the way for Queenside castling. The Queen on "d6" can be easily shifted to a potentially strong post on the Kingside. Other common book moves, which take care of White's threat on the "e" Pawn, are 5…Bg4 and 5…f6.

6 c3

This move prepares support for placing a Pawn in the center on "d4". However, as you will see in the game, this plan allows Black to play aggressively and take advantage of the hole White has created on "d3". Better and more common moves here for White are 6 d4 or 6 d3.

6…Bg4

Black develops his Bishop and pins White's Knight. The Knight on "f3" would have helped support 7 d4. This also allows Black to castle Queenside.

7 h3

This forces White's hand by attacking the Bishop and forcing it to either retreat or be exchanged for the Knight on "f3". If White played 7 d4 Black has tremendous pressure on White's Pawn center after 7…0-0-0.

7...Bxf3

Black removes White's Knight and Queen from supporting the natural thrust in the center with 8 d4. However, maintaining the pin on the Knight with 7...Bh5 was also playable.

8 Qxf3

Diagram 87. Position after 8 Qxf3

White recovers the minor piece. White certainly did not want to play 8 gxf3, exposing his King and getting doubled "f" Pawns. Black could have then played 8...Qd3 and White would have great difficulty in developing his pieces.

8...0-0-0

Black offers a Pawn so that he can get his King out of the center and bring his Rook onto the half-open "d" file. This takes advantage of White's backward "d" Pawn.

9 Qxf7

White accepts Black's Pawn sacrifice. A reasonable alternative for White would have been for him to sacrifice his "d" Pawn with 9 d4. This would have allowed White to free his Queenside pieces.

9...Nf6

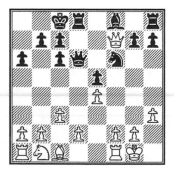

Diagram 88. Position after 9...Nf6

Black develops his Knight toward the center and restricts the squares that White's Queen can retreat to. Although the Knight attacks White's "e" Pawn he doesn't threaten 10...Nxe4?? because of the fork with 11 Qf5+.

10 Qc4?

White defends his "e" Pawn with the Queen, which wasn't necessary. Retreating the Queen doesn't improve her effectiveness. White would have done better to bring his Rook into play and permanently defend the "e" Pawn with 10 Re1. Another reasonable alternative would have been for White to free his Queenside pieces and return the Pawn with 10 d4.

10...b5

This move will help restrain White's Queenside Pawns later on, making it more difficult for him to free his pieces. White must now get his Queen out of attack.

11 Qe2

White gets his Queen out of attack while maintaining her protection of the "e" Pawn.

11...Qd3

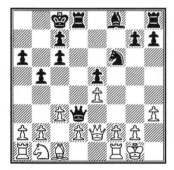

Diagram 89. Position after 11...Qd3

The weakness of having played 6 c3 is clearly demonstrated by this move. Black blockades the advance of White's "d" Pawn by occupying the hole on "d3" and threatens White's Queen.

12 Re1

White brings his Rook into play while defending his Queen and adding protection to his "e" Pawn.

12...Bc5

Black develops his Bishop to the long "g1-a7" diagonal. The pressure this puts on White's "f" Pawn will prove to be very effective later on.

13 b4

White is doing the best he can to free his Queenside pieces while attacking Black's Bishop on "c5".

13...Bb6

Black gets his Bishop out of attack while maintaining it along the effective "g1-a7" diagonal.

14 Qxd3

White tries to relieve the pressure by trading off the Queens.

14...Rxd3

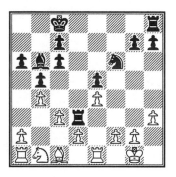

Diagram 90. Position after 14...Rxd3

Black recovers the Queen and clearly has more than enough compensation for the sacrificed Pawn. After he brings his Rook on "h8" into play he will have all of his pieces actively posted. The blockade on White's "d" Pawn greatly restricts White's ability to develop his pieces effectively. At this point all of White's pieces are on his 1st rank!

15 Na3

White develops his Knight to its only available square. Again, as a general rule, *"A Knight on the rim is dim, its chances are very slim."* White plans to maneuver it toward a more centralized square where it will be more effectively posted.

15...Rhf8

This brings Black's last piece into play. The Rook is placed on a half-open file with the idea of eventually increasing pressure on White's weak Pawn on "f2".

A very good alternative for Black would have been to play 15...c5. The idea behind this move would be either to eliminate Black's doubled "c" Pawns or to advance the Pawn to "c4", furthering Black's control of the "d3" square.

16 Nc2

White begins to maneuver the Knight toward the center where it will be more actively located and block Black's strong Bishop along the "g1-a7" diagonal.

16...Nh5

Black temporarily places his Knight on the edge of the board with the plan of posting it on the active "f4" square. Black also threatens to play 17...Bxf2+.

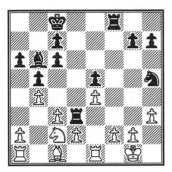

Diagram 91. Position after 16...Nh5

17 Ne3

White completes his Knight maneuver and defends against Black's threat on the "f" Pawn.

17...Nf4

The Knight is actively posted on "f4" where it helps to control the important "d3" square.

18 a4

White seeks counterplay on the Queenside, threatening to open up the "a" file for his Rook with 19 axb5. If White had tried to gain counterplay on the Kingside by attacking Black's "e" Pawn with 18 Ng4 Black could have taken advantage of White's pinned "f" Pawn and played 18...Rg3!, threatening moves like 19...Rxg2+ and 19...Nxh3+.

18...Kb7

This prevents White's Rook from penetrating on the "a" file in the event this file is opened.

19 c4?

Diagram 92. Position after 19 c4

White now threatens to shut out Black's Bishop with 20 c5. However, this opens up lines to Black's favor. Either consolidating on the Kingside and getting the King off of the "g1-a7" diagonal with 19 Kh2, or covering the 2nd rank and adding protection to the backward "d" Pawn with 19 Ra2, were better alternatives.

19...bxc4

This eliminates White's threat of 20 c5. Another good alternative was to post the Bishop actively while attacking White's Rook with 19...Bd4.

20 Ra2

White adds protection to his weak Pawn on "d2" and allows for the possibility of attacking Black's Pawn on "c4" with the Rook going to "c2". If White played 20 Nxc4? see if you can find Black's best move here without looking at the next move.

After 20 Nxc4? Black can play 20...Nxg2!, and if 21 Kxg2 then Rxf2+ 22 Kg1 Rg3+ 23 Kh1 Rxh3+ 24 Kg1 Rg3+ 25 Kh1 Rf4 and mate will soon follow.

20...Rd4

Black opens up "d3" for possible use by his Knight, attacks White's Pawn on "e4" and defends his own Pawn on "c4".

21 Ba3

Diagram 93. Position after 21 Ba3

White finally gets his Bishop developed and removes it from becoming a target to Black's Knight when it goes to "d3".

21...Rfd8

Black shifts his Rook from the "f" file to focus increasing pressure on White's weak "d" Pawn.

22 Nf1

This defends the "d" Pawn against Black's threat of 22...Rxd2.

22...Rd3

Black repositions his Rook, ties down White's Rook to the defense of the Bishop on "a3", opens up the Bishop on the "g1-a7" diagonal, and allows for the possibility of the Rook going to "b3".

23 Bb2

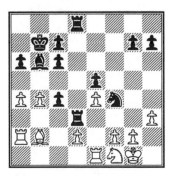

Diagram 94. Position after 23 Bb2

White tries to get counterplay by attacking Black's "e" Pawn. Black now has a couple of nice ways to win. See if you can find one of the winning moves Black can play here without looking at the next move in the game.

23...Rxd2!

Black temporarily sacrifices the exchange, which allows him to penetrate to his 7th rank and force the issue. Also winning, but less dynamic, would have been to play 23...Rb3 planning to meet 24 Bc3 with 24...Nd3.

24 Nxd2

White has nothing better to do than accept Black's exchange sacrifice.

24...Rxd2

Black captures a Knight while posting his Rook strongly on his 7th rank and pinning White's Bishop. Black's biggest threat here is to play 25...Bxf2+ forking White's King and Rook.

25 Rea1

White removes his Rook from being exposed to attack on "e1" by a Bishop fork on "f2". This also defends White's Rook on "a2" and unpins his Bishop.

25...c3

Diagram 95. Position after 25...c3

Black advances his passed Pawn while threatening White's Bishop. Black could have also won easily by going Pawn grabbing with 25...Rxf2.

26 Ba3

White gets his Bishop out of attack. If White played 26 Bxc3 then Black would fork the King and Bishop with 26...Ne2+.

26...c2

Black's Pawn continues its advance, which will soon force the win of material.

27 Kh2

White removes his King from being exposed to possible attacks with 28...Bxf2+ or 28...Rd1+.

27...Nd3

Black's Knight is brought to a more active post covering the Queening square of his passed Pawn.

28 f3

White gets his "f" Pawn out of attack. However, White would have lasted longer by blockading Black's "c" Pawn with 28 Bc1. Black would then do best to play 28...Rxf2.

28...Rd1

Diagram 96. Position after 28...Rd1

This forces the win of material. White is helpless against Black's threat of 29...Bd4 attacking the Rook on "a1". White resigned.

The Use of Open Files in a Kingside Attack

Klaus Junge versus Rudolf Teschner
Correspondence, December 1942–April 1944

Opening: Ruy Lopez

Klaus Junge was born in Chile to German parents in 1924. In 1928 his family moved to Germany where he was to have a brief yet brilliant chess career. He started having respectable results against Masters at the age of 13 and was soon to be a threat to some of the world's top players. He was killed in action during the last remaining days of World War Two.

Rudolf Teschner, born in 1922, was an International Master and West German Champion in 1951.

Black misses a couple of good opportunities to stop White's build-up on the Kingside. Then White is given the opportunity to demonstrate how to effectively use open files in a Kingside attack.

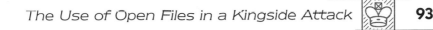

1 e4 e5 2 Nf3 Nc6 3 Bb5 a6 4 Ba4

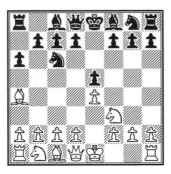

Diagram 97. Position after 4 Ba4

White gets his Bishop out of attack and maintains pressure along the "a4-e8" diagonal. Black must always keep in mind the possibility of White exchanging his Bishop for Black's Knight on "c6" followed by White capturing the "e" Pawn with Nxe5.

4...Nf6

Black develops his Knight toward the center with an attack on White's "e" Pawn.

5 0-0

Diagram 98. Position after 5 0-0

White gets his King out of the center and brings his Rook into play. You will see in this game why White doesn't have to directly defend his "e" Pawn on this move. White's plan is to get a nice Pawn center by moving his Pawn to "c3" to support the placement of a Pawn on "d4". If White had played 5 Nc3 he would block the use of his "c" Pawn. Also, if White defended his "e" Pawn immediately with 5 d3 he would need to move the same Pawn again if he wanted to place it on the more active "d4" square.

5...Nxe4

This is known as the "Open Variation" of the Ruy Lopez. It is not as popular as 5...Be7, which will be seen in Lesson 11. Black eliminates White's center Pawn. How-

ever, as you will soon see, White will have no problem recovering the Pawn and obtaining a good game.

6 d4

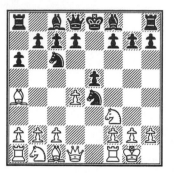

Diagram 99. Position after 6 d4

White boldly attacks in the center and threatens Black's "e" Pawn by attacking it a second time. This also frees the Bishop on "c1", opens up "d2" for possible use by a Knight, and activates the Queen on the "d" file.

If White had played 6 Re1 this would only drive Black's Knight to a good square after 6...Nc5, attacking White's unprotected Bishop on "a4". Therefore, part of White's idea behind playing 6 d4 is to eliminate Black's Pawn on "e5". Once Black's "e" Pawn is removed White can move his Rook to "e1" and Black's Knight would be pinned.

6...b5

Black drives White's Bishop off the "a4-e8" diagonal to avoid having his Knight on "c6" pinned when he advances his "d" Pawn. If Black went Pawn grabbing with 6...exd4 then White would recover one of his Pawns and have pins on both of Black's Knights after 7 Re1 d5 8 Nxd4.

7 Bb3

White gets his Bishop out of attack, moving it to the only available square where it will not be captured.

7...d5

This places a Pawn in the center, defending the Knight on "e4", freeing the Bishop on "c8" and blocking White's Bishop on "b3". Once again if Black goes Pawn grabbing with 7...exd4 White comes out on top after 8 Re1 d5 9 Nc3! dxc3 (if 9...Be6 then 10 Nxe4 dxe4 11 Rxe4 Be7 12 Bxe6 fxe6 13 Nxd4) 10 Bxd5 Bb7 11 Bxe4 Be7 12 Qe2.

8 dxe5

White recovers his Pawn and threatens 9 Bxd5. Playing 8 Nxe5 Nxe5 9 dxe5 would allow Black to defend his "d" Pawn without tying down his Bishop after 9...c6.

8...Be6

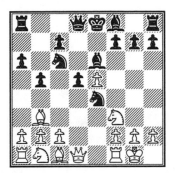

Diagram 100. Position after 8...Be6

Black develops his Bishop and defends his "d" Pawn.

9 c3

This covers the important "d4" square and allows White to reposition his Bishop on "c2". On "c2" the Bishop would increase pressure on Black's Knight on "e4".

9...Be7

Black develops his Bishop to a flexible location and prepares to castle. A more aggressive move here was 9...Bc5. The game might have then continued 10 Nbd2 0-0 11 Bc2 Bf5 (or if 11...Nxf2 12 Rxf2 f6 13 exf6 Bxf2+ 14 Kxf2 Qxf6 15 Nf1 Ne5 16 Be3) 12 Nb3 Bg6 13 Nfd4.

10 Be3

White develops his Bishop to an active location. Also good would have been 10 Nbd2 immediately challenging Black's Knight on "e4".

10...0-0

Black gets his King out of the center and brings a Rook to a more active location.

11 Nbd2

Diagram 101. Position after 11 Nbd2

White develops a Knight toward the center and challenges Black's Knight on "e4".

11...Nxd2

This exchange trades off Black's active Knight and helps White's development. A much stronger move for Black was 11...Qd7. This would have brought Black's Queen to a more active square while connecting his Rooks. White would have then done best to bring his Rook into play and continue his build-up on Black's Knight on "e4" with 12 Re1 Rad8 13 Bc2.

If Black had played actively and pinned White's Knight with 11...Bg4 White would stand better after 12 Nxe4 dxe4 13 Qd5 Qxd5 14 Bxd5 exf3 15 Bxc6 fxg2 16 Kxg2 Rad8 17 a4. Also, if Black tried reinforcing his Knight on "e4" with 11...f5 White would have continued with 12 exf6 e.p. Nxf6 13 Ng5.

12 Qxd2

White recovers his Knight and connects his Rooks.

12...Qd7

This brings Black's Queen to a more active square and connects his Rooks.

13 Rad1

White brings his Rook onto the half-open "d" file and threatens Black's "d" Pawn. However, a stronger idea was to play 13 Qd3 with the idea of provoking Black to weaken the Kingside after 13...Rad8 14 Bc2 g6 15 Rfe1.

13...Rad8

Black brings his Rook to a central file and defends against the threat on his "d" Pawn.

14 Rfe1

Diagram 102. Position after 14 Rfe1

White brings another Rook onto a central file. This will also help reinforce White's actively placed Pawn on "e5".

14...Na5

Black's plan is to seek a more active post for his Knight on "c4" and to try to obtain counterplay on the Queenside by getting his Pawn to "c5".

15 Bc2

White naturally preserves his Bishop pair by not allowing Black to trade his Knight for the Bishop on "b3". The Bishop will be effectively located on the long "b1-h7" diagonal.

15...c5

Black continues with his plan of mobilizing his Pawns on the Queenside and attacks the important "d4" square. If Black immediately attacked White's Queen with 15...Nc4 White would have threatened mate on "h7" with 16 Qd3 and preserved his Bishop pair after 16...g6 17 Bc1.

16 Qd3

This threatens 17 Qxh7++ with the idea of forcing Black to weaken his Kingside.

16...g6

Diagram 103. Position after 16...g6

Black stops White's threat of 17 Qxh7++.

17 Bh6

White begins to take advantage of Black's weakened Kingside by posting his Bishop actively, opening up his Rook on the "e" file and threatening Black's Rook on "f8".

17...Rfe8

Black gets his Rook out of attack, placing it on its only available square.

18 Ng5?

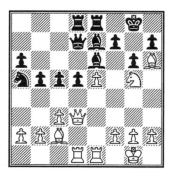

Diagram 104. Position after 18 Ng5

White plays aggressively, trying to immediately go for a Kingside attack. However, he should have taken the time to prevent the entry of Black's Knight to "c4" by playing 18 b3.

18...Nc6?

Black misses his opportunity to post his Knight actively with 18...Nc4. This move would have threatened to win a Pawn and fork the Queen and Rook with 19...Nxb2. White would have completely lost any chances for an initiative on the Kingside.

19 Nxe6

White now obtains the advantage of having the Bishop pair and removes Black's solid defender on "e6".

19...Qxe6

Diagram 105. Position after 19...Qxe6

Black recovers his minor piece while keeping pressure on White's "e" Pawn. If Black played 19...fxe6 White would have a lot of pressure on the Kingside after 20 Qg3 threatening 21 Bxg6.

See if you can find White's best move here without looking at the next move in the game.

20 f4?

White defends his "e" Pawn with his "f" Pawn. Though this idea is correct, the timing is off due to Black's next move in the game. The best move was 20 Qg3!. This would have defended the "e" Pawn with a second piece and prevented Black's next move. Then getting in 21 f4 with the possibility of 22 f5 would have been White's plan.

20...Qg4!

Sometimes a good defense is a good offense! Black actively posts his Queen on the Kingside, which should have neutralized White's attack. Black is now threatening to attack White's Bishop on "h6" with 21...Qh4.

21 Qg3

Swinging the Queen to the Kingside is the only good way to meet Black's threat of 21...Qh4. If White had played 21 Re3 then Black gets the advantage after 21...c4! (attacking White's Queen and threatening to pin the Rook with 22...Bc5) 22 Qe2 Qxe2 23 Rxe2 d4! 24 Be4 d3 25 Ree1 Bc5+ 26 Kf1 Ne7.

21...Qh5

Black still attacks and threatens White's Bishop on "h6". Black could have also simplified the game by trading Queens with 21...Qxg3 22 hxg3 Na5.

22 Bg5

This was White's only good move to get his Bishop out of attack.

22...Bxg5

Black will seek counterplay by doubling White's "g" Pawns and giving White an isolated "e" Pawn.

23 fxg5

Diagram 106. Position after 23 fxg5

White recovers his Bishop.

23...Re6

Black blocks the possible advance of White's "e" Pawn. This move also allows for the possibility of doubling Rooks on the "e" file, which would increase pressure on White's isolated "e" Pawn.

24 Qf4

White attacks the "h6" square again in an attempt to restrain Black from playing 24...h6 and begins to put pressure on Black's "f" Pawn.

24...Kg7?

This is too slow. Black's plan of using his King to help support the advance of his Pawn to "h6" is not necessary. Black could have played 24...h6 right away planning to meet 25 gxh6 with 25...Nxe5. Also, after 24...h6 if White played 25 h4 Black has the neat maneuver 25...hxg5 26 hxg5 Qh8! and Black's "e" Pawn is attacked three times.

25 Rd3!

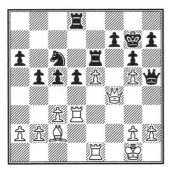

Diagram 107. Position after 25 Rd3

White brings his Rook into play where it can swing over to the "h" file. White is threatening to win Black's Queen with either 26 Bd1 or 26 Rh3. The weakness of Black's 24th move now becomes more apparent.

25...h6

Black attacks White's "g" Pawn with the plan of opening the "h" file and allowing an escape for his Queen.

26 h4

White defends and maintains his strongly posted Pawn on "g5". White now threatens to attack Black's Queen with 27 Bd1.

26...hxg5

Black opens the "h" file to allow for an escape for his Queen.

27 hxg5

White recovers and maintains his strongly posted Pawn on "g5". White now threatens to win Black's Queen with 28 Rh3.

27...Qh8

To avoid being trapped, the Queen retreats.

28 Rh3

White's Rook takes command of the open "h" file while gaining time by attacking Black's Queen. The use of the "h" file will prove very useful in taking advantage of both Black's awkwardly located Queen and Black's exposed King.

28...Qg8

Diagram 108. Position after 28...Qg8

Black gets his Queen out of attack and tries to keep her as active as possible in the defense of the King. White now can force the win of material and continue his build-up on the Kingside with a nice maneuver.

See if you can find White's best move here without looking at the next move in the game.

29 Bd1!

White plans to maneuver his Bishop to "g4" and attack Black's strongly posted Rook.

29...Ne7

Black does his best to defend on the Kingside by preparing to bring his Knight to "f5". See if you can find White's best move here without looking at the next move in the game.

30 Rf1!

White could have attacked Black's Rook with 30 Bg4, winning a Pawn and leaving Black's King exposed after 30...Nf5 31 Bxf5 gxf5 32 Qxf5. However, there was no rush to do this. White first increases the pressure by bringing his Rook into play on the open "f" file before executing his plan of attacking with his Bishop on "g4".

30...Qe8

There is little Black could do to avoid the impending disaster. However, this move serves no purpose and only speeds up the collapse. If Black's King tried to run with 30...Kf8 White can win Black's Queen with 31 Rh8!, planning to meet 31...Qxh8 with 32 Qxf7++. Also, if Black tried to get counterplay with 30...d4, White has a nice Rook sacrifice with 31 Rh7+ Qxh7 (if 31...Kxh7 then 32 Qh4+ Kg7 33 Qh6++) 32 Qxf7+ Kh8 33 Qxe6 winning easily.

31 Bg4

White's Bishop comes into play, attacking Black's Rook.

31...Nf5

Diagram 109. Position after 31...Nf5

Black does the best he can to defend by using his Knight to block White's Bishop. See if you can find White's best move here without looking at the next move in the game.

32 Qh2!

White threatens to win Black's Queen with 33 Rh7+ Kf8 34 Rh8+. White could have won a Pawn with 32 Bxf5 gxf5 33 Qxf5. However after 33...Rg6 it would take longer for White to win.

32...Qg8

Black takes care of White's threat of 33 Rh7+ by attacking "h7" with his Queen.

33 Bxf5

This removes Black's Knight, which blocked the use of the "f" file by White's Rook.

33...gxf5

Black recovers the piece.

34 Rxf5

White wins a Pawn while opening the "f" file for use by his Rook against Black's exposed King.

34...Rd7

There is really nothing for Black to do here. Black adds protection to his "f" Pawn, which does little good against White's many threats.

35 Rh6

Diagram 110. Position after 35...Rh6

Black resigned here. White threatened 36 Rxe6 fxe6 37 Qh6++. If Black had tried 35...Rde7 then White would play 36 Rff6 threatening 37 Rhg6+ (if 37...fxg6, then 38 Qh6++).

The Main Line of the Ruy Lopez

Fischer versus Shocron
Mar del Plata, 1959

Opening: Ruy Lopez

Robert ("Bobby") Fischer was the first American to win the World Chess Championship. When he defeated Boris Spassky during his famous 1972 match in Iceland, he also became the first non-Russian to win the title since 1937. Fischer was born in 1943 and learned to play at the age of eight. In 1958 Fischer won the US Championship and became an International Grandmaster. He went on to win all eight U.S. Championships he played in, including having a perfect 11-0 score in the 1963–64 U.S. Championship.

After winning the World Championship title in 1972, Fischer disappeared from playing in the public for 20 years. In 1992 he defeated Spassky in another match, then he disappeared again! Many people consider Fischer to have been the strongest player in the history of the game.

Fischer was well known for his use and his deep analysis of the Ruy Lopez. Both sides use long range strategic plans to accomplish important goals.

Just as it seemed as if Black was going to hold the game, he faltered and allowed Fischer to use a winning sacrifice.

1 e4 e5 2 Nf3 Nc6 3 Bb5 a6 4 Ba4 Nf6 5 0-0 Be7

Diagram 111. Position after 5...Be7

Black develops his Bishop to a flexible location while shielding his King on the "e" file. As a result, if given the move, Black would obtain a good game by playing 6...Nxe4.

6 Re1

White defends the "e" Pawn and brings his Rook onto a more active file in the center. Other methods of defending the "e" Pawn are inferior. White would like to gain as much space as possible in the center by placing Pawns on "c3" and "d4" and creating an active Pawn chain. Defending the "e" Pawn with 6 Nc3 would block the use of White's "c" Pawn, and playing 6 d3 would be a waste of time if White planned to place the Pawn more actively on "d4".

White could not have won a Pawn with 6 Bxc6 dxc6 7 Nxe5 because of 7...Nxe4. However, now that White's "e" Pawn is defended he is threatening to win a Pawn with 7 Bxc6 dxc6 9 Nxe5.

6...b5

Black drives the Bishop off of the "a5-e8" diagonal, which prevents White from winning a Pawn with 7 Bxc6. The significance of Black playing 3...a6 becomes more apparent now that the "b" Pawn's advance has been supported.

7 Bb3

White gets his Bishop out of attack while placing it on the long "a2-g8" diagonal.

7...d6

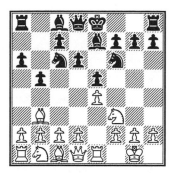

Diagram 112. Position after 7...d6

Black opens up the "c8-h3" diagonal for the Bishop on "c8" and defends his "e" Pawn a second time. Black's Knight is now free to go to "a5" and attack White's good "Lopez" Bishop. In the Ruy Lopez it would be to Black's advantage to exchange a Knight for this good Bishop.

8 c3

White opens up "c2" giving his Bishop a retreat square and supporting the Pawn move "d4". Playing an immediate 8 d4 allows Black to set up the "Noah's Ark Trap" with 8...exd4. If White now plays 9 Nxd4? then Black would have White's Bishop trapped after 9...Nxd4 10 Qxd4 c5 11 Qc3 c4.

8...0-0

Black gets his King out of the center and into safety while bringing his Rook to a more active location.

9 h3

White attacks the "g4" square preventing a possible pin by Black's Bishop. If White had played 9 d4 Black would have pinned White's Knight with 9...Bg4.

9...Na5

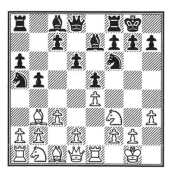

Diagram 113. Position after 9...Na5

Placing a Knight on the edge of the board is usually not a good idea. However Black has two good reasons to violate this general rule. First of all, Black attacks White's good "Lopez" Bishop and drives it off of the long "a2-g8" diagonal. Second, Black can now use his "c" Pawn to attack in the center and expand on the Queenside.

10 Bc2

White retreats the "Lopez" Bishop to prevent Black from trading his Knight for it with 11...Nxb3.

10...c5

Black attacks the important "d4" square a second time, expands on the Queenside and opens up the "a5-d8" diagonal for his Queen.

11 d4

White occupies the center with a Pawn, frees his Queenside minor pieces and threatens Black's "e" Pawn by attacking it a second time.

11...Qc7

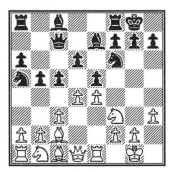

Diagram 114. Position after 11...Qc7

Black brings his Queen to an active post where she aids in the defense of the "e" Pawn and can possibly be used in an attack along the potentially open "c" file.

Another reasonable way for Black to defend the "e" Pawn is 11...Nd7. This is an active alternative known as the "Keres Variation" which I sometimes recommend to my students. Black clears the "f6" square for possible use by a Bishop, and the Knight on "d7" has the option of being used on the Queenside.

After 11...Nd7 White has a couple of main alternatives which will be briefly outlined here:

1.   12 dxc5 (or 12 dxe5) dxc5 13 Nbd2 Bb7 14 Nf1 Nc4, with a comfortable game for Black.

2. 12 Nbd2 cxd4 13 cxd4 Nc6 14 Nf1 (if 14 Nb3 a5 15 Bd3 Ba6 16 d5 Nb4
17 Bf1 a4, or if 14 d5 Nb4 15 Bb1 a5) exd4 15 Nxd4 Nxd4 16 Qxd4 Ne5
threatening 17…Bxh3. Black has active pieces as compensation for his isolated
"d" Pawn.

12 Nbd2

White develops his Knight toward the center. Even though the Knight on "d2"
blocks the development of White's Bishop on "c1" this is only temporary. White's plan
is to maneuver his Knight via "f1" to an active post on "e3".

12…Bd7

Black develops his Bishop to a flexible post where it covers both sides of the board
and connects his Rooks on his 1st rank. If he had developed the Bishop to a more aggressive post with 12…Be6, the Bishop would have been a target for a Pawn going to
"d5" or a Knight going to "g5". Developing the Bishop with 12…Bb7 would allow
White to block the Bishop's "h1-a8" diagonal by placing a Pawn on "d5". Also the
Bishop would be removed from the useful "h3-c8" diagonal if developed to "b7".

13 Nf1

White's Knight continues its maneuver toward the Kingside and reopens the "c1-
h6" diagonal for the Bishop on "c1".

13…Rfe8

Black brings his Rook to a central file where it helps to strengthen the center and
add support to the "e" Pawn. This move also opens up "f8" for possible use by Black's
Bishop.

14 Ne3

The Knight is brought to a flexible central location where it attacks critical squares
on "c4", "d5", "f5" and "g4". The Bishop on "c1" is once again blocked on the "c1-h6"
diagonal, however, the benefits of having such a strongly posted Knight outweighs
this temporary disadvantage. To find the proper placement of the Bishop on "c1"consider the following general opening rule:*"If it is unclear where it is best to develop a
piece then consider delaying its development until things become clearer."*

14...g6

Diagram 115. Position after 14...g6

This move has a lot of good reasons behind it. First, it will keep White's Knight out of "f5". Second, it will allow for the repositioning of Black's Bishop once it goes to "f8" by then having the "g7" and "h6" squares available to it. Third, it creates "luft", a breathing square for Black's King, by opening up "g7", which reduces the possibility of a back-rank mate later in the game. And fourth, it will protect Black's Knight on "h5" if Black should want to maneuver it via "h5" to "f4". The weakness on the dark squares that this move creates is minor compared to all of the benefits it provides.

15 dxe5

White increases the possibility of his Knight entering the outpost on "d5" while eliminating the possibility of Black playing cxd4. A less active move would have been to develop his Bishop with 15 Bd2. Black's best move would have been 15...Bf8, opening up the Rook on the "e" file and allowing the Bishop to be repositioned on the Kingside.

15...dxe5

Black recaptures his Pawn.

16 Nh2

White temporarily places his Knight on a less active square. However, White's plan is to post the Knight on the very aggressive "g4" square in the near future. This move also opens up the "f3" square for use by White's Queen as part of a thematic plan to build up on the Kingside.

16...Rad8

Black brings his Rook onto an open file in the center while threatening a discovered attack on White's Queen with 17...Bxh3.

17 Qf3

Diagram 116. Position after 17 Qf3

White's Queen gets off of the "d" file and puts pressure on Black's Knight on "f6". This fits in well with White's plan of bringing a Knight to "g4".

17...Be6

Black places his bishop on the more active "a2-g8" diagonal, prepares support for his Knight to enter "c4" and opens up the "d" file for his Rook.

18 Nhg4

White continues his build-up on the Kingside, bringing his Knight back into play and threatening Black's Knight on "f6".

18...Nxg4

Black eliminates White's threat on his Knight on "f6" by trading it off.

19 hxg4

White recovers his Knight while opening up the "h" file for possible use by a Rook. Black will need to defend carefully. The Pawn on "g4" may also assist in a possible attack. Though 19 Nxg4 was also playable, White has few prospects of getting attacking chances on the Kingside after 19...Bxg4.

19...Qc6

Black removes his Queen from a square where she would be attacked if White's Knight goes to "d5". An excellent alternative here would have been for Black to bring his Knight actively into play and challenge White's Knight with 19...Nc4. After 20 Nd5 Bxd5 21 exd5 Nb6 the game would be about even.

20 g5

Diagram 117. Position after 20 g5

White opens up "g4" for use by his Knight and attacks both Black's weak "f6" and "h6" squares with his Pawn. However, this move offers a rather speculative sacrifice. Therefore, 20 Qg3 attacking Black's Pawn on "e5" and defending the pawn on "g5" would have been a good alternative.

20...Nc4

Black brings his Knight to a more active post with the plan of simplifying by exchanging Knights on "e3". It would have been reasonable for Black to have accepted White's Pawn sacrifice with 20...Bxg5. After 21 Nd5 Black would have a couple of choices.

After 20...Bxg5 21 Nd5 Black could get two Pawns and a Knight for a Rook after 21...Bh4 22 g3 Rxd5 23 exd5 Bxd5 24 Be4 Bxe4 25 Qxe4 Qxe4 26 Rxe4 Bf6. As a general rule, *"A minor piece and two Pawns are superior to a Rook."* However, in this case because there are Pawns on both sides of the board and Black has a Knight for the Rook Black's advantage is minimal at best. As a general rule, *"A bishop is superior to a Knight in an endgame where there are Pawns on both sides of the board."* Knights are short-range pieces and have difficulty in handling a situation that requires them to be used on both sides of the board at the same time. As a general rule, *"Knights are natural-born blockaders of Pawns and do well in closed positions."*

Another option after 20...Bxg5 21 Nd5 is to play 21...Bxc1. After 22 Nf6+ Kh8 23 Raxc1 Rf8 the game is approximately even.

21 Ng4

White avoids trading Knights while posting his Knight strongly on the Kingside attacking Black's weak "f6" and "h6" squares.

21...Bxg4

Black is smart to exchange his Bishop for White's very active Knight.

22 Qxg4

Diagram 118. Position after 22 Qxg4

White recovers his minor piece. An evaluation of this position and what the strategies of each player are will now be pointed out.

White has a spatial advantage on the Kingside where his "g" Pawn cramps Black and his Queen is actively posted. White will try to attack Black's weak point on "h7" and use the open "h" file to carry out his plan. Though it may appear that White is underdeveloped on the Queenside, his Bishop on "c1" already helps to exert pressure on the Kingside and White's Rook has the possibility of being activated by the timely move of a Pawn to "a4".

Black, on the other hand, has a spatial advantage on the Queenside and connected Rooks already located on the two center files. Black has a most interesting plan available to him to defend his weak point on "h7". He will maneuver his Knight to "f8"!

See if you can find Black's best move here without looking at the next move in the game.

22...Nb6!

Not only does this move prevent White from playing 23 a4, it is the beginning of the Knight's journey to "f8" where it will defend the weak "h7" square. Playing 22...f6 would have isolated and weakened Black's "e" Pawn after 23 gxf6. After 23...Bxf6 White would also be able to counterattack on the Queenside with 24 a4.

23 g3

This opens up the "g2" square for White's King, which is in theme with White's plan to get his Rook to "h1" to attack along the "h" file.

23...c4

Black continues with his plan of expanding on the Queenside where he has opportunities for counterplay. This move further opens the "a3-f8" diagonal for his

Bishop and covers the important "b3" and "d3" squares. If Black had continued his Knight maneuver immediately with 23…Nd7 then White could have counter-punched with 24 a4.

24 Kg2

This gives White's Rook access to the "h1" square.

24…Nd7

Black now continues with his Knight maneuver toward "f8". However, Black has the option of switching his plan and posting the Knight very actively on "c5". This idea makes 25 a4 less attractive to White since it would weaken "b3" and Black's Knight would attack both "b3 and "a4" from "c5".

25 Rh1

White brings his Rook to the open "h" file putting pressure on Black's "h" Pawn.

25…Nf8

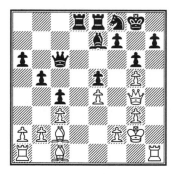

Diagram 119. Position after 25…Nf8

Black completes his plan of covering his weakness on "h7". The Knight on "f8" also has the distant possibility of springing back into play by going to "e6". Now that Black has defended adequately on the Kingside White takes action to restrain and limit Black's possibilities on the Queenside.

26 b4

White counters on the Queenside instead of passively waiting for Black to continue his expansion there.

26…Qe6

Black repositions his Queen offering a favorable Queen trade. A reasonable alternative would have been 26…a5 planning to meet 27 bxa5 with 27…Qa6. If Black went Pawn grabbing with 26…cxb3 e.p. 27 Bxb3 Qxc3 White gets a great position after 28 Be3 with more than enough compensation for his sacrificed Pawn. However, after 26...cxb3 e.p. 27 Bxb3 then posting the Rook actively with 27...Rd3 would have given Black a reasonable game.

27 Qe2

White is wise to avoid trading Queens. If White had traded Queens with 27 Qxe6 Black's Knight would have come actively into play after 27...Nxe6. White places his Queen on the most active and flexible square available.

27...a5

Black continues with his general plan of opening up lines and expanding on the Queenside.

28 bxa5

White will force Black to take the time to recover his Pawn. An interesting idea for White would have been to complicate matters with 28 a4.

28...Qa6

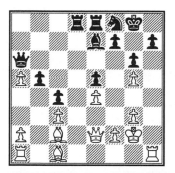

Diagram 120. Position after 28...Qa6

Black brings his Queen actively into play on the Queenside and prepares to recover the Pawn that he temporarily sacrificed.

29 Be3

White finally develops his last minor piece, placing it as actively as possible.

29...Qxa5

Black recovers his sacrificed Pawn with an attack on White's isolated "c" Pawn.

30 a4

White begins to break up Black's Pawns by attacking the base of the Pawn chain. By attacking Black's Pawn on "b5" White weakens Black's Pawn on "c4". As a general rule, *"The weakest point of a Pawn chain is at the base."* This move also activates White's Rook on "a1".

30...Ra8?

Black misses his opportunity to maintain equality. Shifting his Rook to the "a" file is too slow. Black should have played more actively with 30...Qxc3 31 axb5 Ne6 and the Knight is heading for the strong outpost on "d4".

31 axb5

White continues with his plan of breaking up Black's Pawn chain and weakening Black's Pawn on "c4".

31...Qxb5

Diagram 121. Position after 31...Qxb5

Black recovers his Pawn. If Black had played 31...Qxc3 White would obtain a clear advantage after 32 Ba4! White has moves like 33 b6 or 33 Rhc1 coming in.

32 Rhb1

White brings his Rook into play on the Queenside where the action is. Black must now get his Queen out of attack.

32...Qc6

Black gets his Queen out of attack while maintaining protection of his "c" Pawn.

33 Rb6

White penetrates with his Rook while gaining time by attacking Black's Queen. This is part of White's plan to gain control of the "a" file.

33...Qc7

Black gets his Queen out of attack again while maintaining protection of his "c" Pawn. If Black played 33...Qxb6 he would have lost a Pawn after 34 Rxa8! Qc6 35 Rxe8 Qxe8 36 Qxc4.

34 Rba6

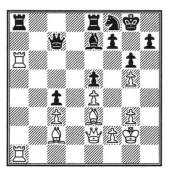

Diagram 122. Position after 34 Rba6

White continues with his plan of gaining control of the "a" file.

34...Rxa6

Black takes care of the threat on his Rook by making an even exchange and minimizing his loss of time. If 34...Rab8 then White would have penetrated to the 7th rank and attacked Black's Queen with 35 Ra7.

35 Rxa6

White recovers his Rook.

35...Rc8

Black realizes that his "c" Pawn is a target and his Queen is its only defender. Black therefore uses his Rook to assist with the protection of the "c" Pawn. As a general rule, *"When you have a choice of tying down a weaker or a stronger piece to perform a defensive task it is better to use the weaker piece."*

36 Qg4

White gives up his direct pressure on Black's "c" Pawn to reposition his Queen on the open "h3-c8" diagonal. A good alternative would have been to immediately bring the Bishop into play along the "a4-e8" diagonal with 36 Ba4.

36...Ne6?

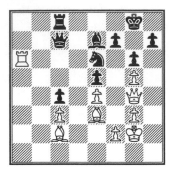

Diagram 123. Position after 36...Ne6

Black overlooks a strong sacrifice for White. Black is trying to get his Knight back into play. Under the circumstances Black should have tried to simplify as much as possible with 36...Bc5 37 Bxc5 Qxc5. However, after 38 Ba4 White is clearly better.

37 Ba4?

White misses his opportunity to sacrifice the exchange with 37 Rxe6! After 37...fxe6 38 Qxe6+ followed by 39 Bb6 Black is in serious trouble. For example after 38...Kf8 39 Bb6 Qb8 40 Ba4 with the idea of 41 Bd7 is devastating.

37...Rb8

Black seeks counterplay by locating his Rook on the open "b" file. Black also avoids giving White another opportunity to sacrifice his Rook on "e6" by removing his Rook from its exposed location on "c8".

38 Rc6

Diagram 124. Position after 38 Rc6

White attacks Black's Queen and weak "c" Pawn.

38...Qd8?

This allows White to use a winning exchange sacrifice. Black missed his opportunity to play 38...Qd7, which would have defended the Knight on "e6" and use a pin to reduce the activity of White's Rook. In this case White would have had very little advantage. If 39 Rxc4? then 39...Qd3! 40 Rc6 Rb1 and Black has a strong attack due to both his Queen and Rook attacking the "f1" square.

39 Rxe6!

This exchange sacrifice exposes Black's King and pieces to a deadly attack.

39...Qc8

Diagram 125. Position after 39...Qc8

Black takes his best practical chance by pinning the Rook to the Queen and forcing White to play brilliantly! Black realized he was losing badly with no chances of survival after 39...fxe6 40 Qxe6+ Kf8 41 Qxe5 Kf7 42 Bd4.

See if you can find White's best move here without looking at the next move in the game.

40 Bd7!

Black cannot take the Bishop with 40...Qxd7 due to a discovered attack, which wins his Queen after 41 Rxg6+ hxg6 42 Qxd7. Black resigned, as he would be a piece and a Pawn down after 40...Qd8 41 Rxe5.

l e s s o n

12

Awesome Pieces

Anatoly Karpov versus Boris Spassky
Moscow, 1973

Opening: Ruy Lopez

Anatoly Karpov (World Champion 1975–1985) was awarded a cut crystal bowl for this game in the 1973 USSR National Teams Match Tournament. Born in Zlatoust, Russia, in 1951, Karpov was declared World Champion in 1975 when Bobby Fischer refused to defend his title.

Even though you will find that Boris Spassky (World Champion 1969–1972) didn't win any of his games in this book, he was worthy of his World Championship title and a true gentleman. I met him in San Francisco, California in 1980 when he wanted me to be one of his trainers in his preparations to try for the World Championship once again. Born in Leningrad, Russia in 1937, Spassky is most famous for having lost his World Championship title in 1972 to Bobby Fischer.

This game shows the importance of long range planning to effectively coordinate your pieces. To this end White doesn't mind giving up the exchange to overwhelm Black's position.

1 e4 e5 2 Nf3 Nc6 3 Bb5 a6 4 Ba4 Nf6 5 0-0 Be7 6 Re1 b5
7 Bb3 d6 8 c3 0-0 9 h3 Nb8

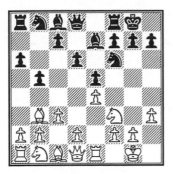

Diagram 126. Position after 9...Nb8

This is known as the Breyer variation of the Ruy Lopez. Black temporarily retreats his Knight with the plan of redeploying it on "d7" where the Knight will add protection to Black's "e" Pawn and will have the option of coming into play on "c5". This extremely positional approach to the Ruy Lopez has been a favorite of both Karpov and Spassky.

10 d3

White frees his Bishop on "c1", opens up "d2" for use by his Knight and defends his "e" Pawn again. Since Black will likely attack the "e" Pawn a second time by developing his Bishop to "b7" this move makes sense for White. A more aggressive line here was 10 d4 Nbd7 11 Nbd2 Bb7 12 Bc2 Re8 13 Nf1 Bf8 14 Ng3 g6 15 a4.

10...Bb7

Black fianchettos his Bishop increasing his pressure on White's "e" Pawn.

11 Nbd2

White develops his Knight with the plan of maneuvering it to the Kingside.

11...Nbd7

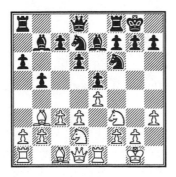

Diagram 127. Position after 11...Nbd7

Black continues with his plan of redeploying his Knight.

12 Nf1

White continues maneuvering his Knight toward the Kingside.

12...Nc5

Black's Knight is actively posted on "c5" where it attacks White's important "Lopez" Bishop on "b3" and increases the pressure on White's "e" Pawn.

13 Bc2

White naturally avoids allowing Black to exchange his Knight for the "Lopez" Bishop.

13...Re8

Black brings his Rook onto a central file where it will help reinforce the "e" Pawn. The other idea behind this move is to allow Black's Bishop to go to "f8" which helps to open the Rook on the "e" file and potentially relocate the Bishop on "g7". This game is a good illustration of high-quality positional play.

14 Ng3

White brings his Knight into play on the Kingside attacking the critical "f5" square and aiding in the protection of his "e" Pawn. Playing 14 Ne3 would block White's Rook from defending the "e" Pawn and hinder his plan of playing "d4".

14...Bf8

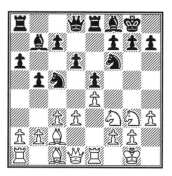

Diagram 128. Position after 14...Bf8

In theme with relocating his Bishop and increasing the effectiveness of his Rook, Black continues using a positional approach to improve the location of his pieces.

15 b4

White drives Black's Knight back from its active post. White's plan is to take away some of the pressure on his "e" Pawn in preparation for the natural "d4" thrust. However, there would have been nothing wrong with simply completing his minor piece development with 15 Be3.

15...Ncd7

Black gets his Knight out of attack while placing it on a square where it can be brought to an even more active post on the Queenside. Black now threatens to gain a stronger foothold in the center with 16...d5.

It may appear on the surface that 15...Ne6 was more active. However, it would block the use of Black's Rook on the "e" file and wouldn't threaten to strike at the center with the "d" Pawn. Also, the Knight wouldn't have an immediate opportunity to go to an even stronger post like the text move allows.

16 d4

White strikes at the center first, preventing Black from playing 16...d5. White's spatial advantage gives him the edge in this position.

16...h6

This move creates an unnecessary weakness on the Kingside, however for some reason it has been considered a main book line! It would have been better for Black to reposition the Knight with 16...Nb6 or play 16...g6 with the idea of fianchettoing the Bishop on "g7".

17 Bd2

White completes his minor piece development and adds protection to his "b" Pawn. However, 17 a4 would have been an excellent alternative, putting more immediate pressure on Black.

17...Nb6

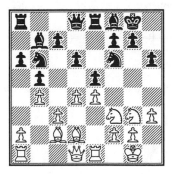

Diagram 129. Position after 17...Nb6

This is an excellent post for the Knight, covering the important "a4", "c4" and "d5" squares.

18 Bd3

White attacks the hole on "c4", prevents the possible advance of Black's "a" Pawn by tying it down to the defense of his "b" Pawn and opens up "c2" for use by his Queen.

18...g6

Black prepares to fianchetto his Bishop on "g7".

19 Qc2

White opens up "d1" for use by a Rook and uses his Queen to help protect his "e" Pawn.

19...Nfd7

Black's Knight on "d7" will help support his natural counter thrust with "c5". This move also will increase the effectiveness of Black's Bishop on the "a1-h8" diagonal when it is positioned on "g7".

20 Rad1

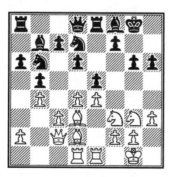

Diagram 130. Position after 20 Rad1

White brings his Rook to a central file, which is likely to be opened up in the future.

20...Bg7

Black completes his fianchetto and allows the Bishop to directly exert pressure in the center.

21 dxe5

The usual plans of trying to build up on the Kingside or break with "f4" would be too slow and awkward for White. Black would likely be able to counter with "d5". Therefore, this exchange in the center prevents Black from playing "d5".

21...dxe5

It would have been better to simplify and trade Knights with 21...Nxe5.

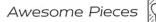

22 c4

White strikes at the center first before Black gets in "c5".

22...bxc4

Black eliminates White's menacing "c" Pawn.

23 Bxc4

Diagram 131. Position after 23 Bxc4

White recovers his Pawn.

23...Qe7?

Black misses his opportunity play 23...Nxc4 to obtain the Bishop pair as partial compensation for his isolated Pawns and less active pieces.

24 Bb3!

White prevents Black from getting the Bishop pair with 24...Nxc4. With this move White prepares to sacrifice the exchange to obtain awesome piece play. White would have also had a nice advantage by playing more conservatively with 24 Be2, but the text is more forcing.

24...c5

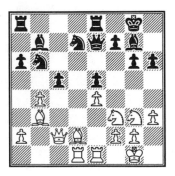

Diagram 132. Position after 24...c5

Black strikes at the center threatening 25...cxb4 and 25...c4. See if you can find White's best move here without looking at the next move in the game.

25 a4!

White opens up "a2" for his Bishop and plans to drive back Black's Knight with "a5". As previously mentioned, White has also decided to take a road leading to an exchange sacrifice.

25...c4

Black drives back and temporarily blocks out White's active Bishop. This will weaken White's defense of his Pawn on "a4" which will allow Black to force the win of material. However, this is all part of White's plan!

26 Ba2

White gets his Bishop out of attack.

26...Bc6

Black threatens White's "a" Pawn and sets up a skewer along the "a4-d1" diagonal.

27 a5

White gets his "a" Pawn out of attack and will drive back Black's Knight.

27...Ba4

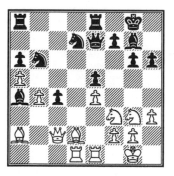

Diagram 133. Position after 27...Ba4

Black skewers White's Queen and Rook, which wins the exchange. At a glance it may appear that White has problems. However, a closer look at the position will reveal it is Black who is in trouble.

28 Qc1

White's pieces are all in play and actively posted. White has threats on Black's Knight on "b6", which will be driven back to an inferior square, and against Black's Pawns on "c4" and "h6". Black's pieces, on the other hand, are poorly coordinated.

28...Nc8

Black gets his Knight out of attack, retreating it to its only available square. Since White's Rook on "d1" isn't going anywhere, there was no rush to capture it.

29 Bxh6

White gets a Pawn for his exchange sacrifice right off the bat while stripping the Black King of part of his Pawn shield. There was no rush to capture White's weak Pawn on "c4" since its future is doomed. White also opens up his Rook on the "d" file, which will tie down Black's Queen to the defense of his Knight on "d7".

29...Bxd1

Black needs to accept White's exchange sacrifice before the Rook escapes and Black ends up with a bad position without any compensation.

30 Rxd1

Diagram 134. Position after 30 Rxd1

White recaptures, bringing his other Rook onto the open "d" file. A close look at the position clearly reveals that, due to all of White's pieces being actively in play, he has more than enough compensation for his exchange sacrifice.

30...Nd6?

This move loses quickly due to an unexpected series of moves White has that will take advantage of Black's two Knights along the "d" file. It would have been better to

play 30...Nf8 relieving Black's Queen from the burden of defending the Knight on "d7". See if you can find White's best move here without looking at the next move in the game.

31 Bxg7

As part of White's plan he exchanges Bishops, which frees his Queen from having to defend the Bishop on "h6".

31...Kxg7

Diagram 135. Position after 31...Kxg7

Black recovers his Bishop. See if you can find White's best move here without looking at the next move in the game.

32 Qg5!

Surprise! White unexpectedly offers an exchange of Queens. However, if Black trades Queens with 32...Qxg5 after 33 Nxg5 one of his Knights would be lost due to the attack along the "d" file. White is now threatening to win a piece with 33 Rxd6, as Black cannot recapture with 33...Qxd6 due to 34 Nf5+ forking the King and Queen.

32...f6

Black avoids a Queen exchange, but now White has an overwhelming attack.

33 Qg4

White's Queen is relocated to a very strong attacking post with White's biggest threat once again being 34 Rxd6. Not as strong, but still winning, would have been 33 Qd2 forcing the win of material.

33 . . . Kh7

Diagram 136. Position after 33...Kh7

Black unpins his "g" Pawn, which relieves White's threat of 34 Rxd6. However, it did nothing to stop White's secondary threat.

See if you can find White's best move here without looking at the next move in the game.

34 Nh4!

Black resigns. Attempts by Black to defend his "g" Pawn would be hopeless. Let's take a look as some of these attempts,

1. 34...Nf8 35 Nxg6! Nxg6 36 Rxd6 Qxd6 (if 36...Kh8 then 37 Rd7!) 37 Qh5+ Kg8 38 Qxg6+ Kf8 39 Nf5 Qd1+ 40 Kh2 Re6 41 Bxc4 and the curtain drops.

2. 34...Rg8 35 Rxd6 (35 Bxc4 also wins) Qxd6 36 Nhf5 gxf5 37 Qh5+ Kg7 38 Nxf5+ forking the King and Queen.

3. 34...g5 35 Rxd6 Qxd6 36 Ngf5 Qf8 37 Qh5+ Kg8 38 Bxc4+ and mate soon follows.

lesson

13

Masters Blunder, Too

Snyder (USA) versus Khasoff (France)
ICCF Master Class, 1977

Opening: Caro-Kann Defense

This game is a good example of how a Master can overlook one critical move, which results in immediate devastation. The Caro-Kann Defense is considered to be a rather conservative but solid defense. However, a player should be well prepared before using it because it is loaded with traps and easy ways for Black to go wrong.

1 e4 c6

Diagram 137. Position after 2...c6

Black initiates the Caro-Kann Defense. With "c6" Black prepares support for the "d" Pawn to counter in the center with 2...d5. The Caro-Kann Defense usually gives White a spatial advantage in the center. One of Black's long-term plans is to entice White to push too hard to get an advantage and overextend himself. This may result in weaknesses in White's Pawn structure, which would give Black a superior endgame.

2 d4

I tell my students as a general rule, *"If Black doesn't immediately challenge you in the center after 1 e4 (e.g. playing 1...b6, 1...c6, 1...d6, 1...e6, or 1...g6), then take command of the center with 2 d4."* This occupies the center with a second Pawn and frees the Bishop on "c1".

2...d5

Black follows through with his plan of countering in the center, freeing his Bishop on "c8" and opening up "d7" for possible use by a Knight. Black now threatens to capture White's Pawn on "e4".

3 Nc3

Diagram 138. Position after 3 Nc3

White develops his Knight toward the center and defends his Pawn on "e4". Advancing the Pawn with 3 e5 allows Black to obtain a comfortable game after 3...Bf5 4 Nf3 e6 5 Be2 c5.

3...dxe4

Because of the pressure on Black's Pawn on "d5" it was difficult for Black to find a good way to continue with his development. Therefore, this exchange eliminates the pressure and allows Black to choose from several plans of development.

4 Nxe4

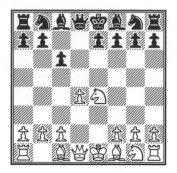

Diagram 139. Position after 4 Nxe4

White recovers the Pawn and brings his Knight to an active central post. Black will usually try to take advantage of the fact that the Knight is undefended to gain time for his own development.

4...Nd7

This is one of several main opening lines for Black here. Black develops his Knight to "d7" where it will support his other Knight going to "f6". When Black develops his Knight to "f6", if White's Knight captures, Black will be able to avoid getting doubled Pawns by recapturing with his Knight on "d7".

If Black plays an immediate 4...Nf6 White gets a good game by giving Black doubled Pawns after 5 Nxf6+. Black would have two ways to recapture. Possible continuations are:

1. 5...exf6 6 Bc4 Bd6 7 Qe2+ Qe7 8 Qxe7+ Kxe7 9 Ne2 and White's Queenside Pawn majority gives him the edge.
2. 5...gxf6 6 c3 Bf5 7 Ne2 (7 Nf3 is also playable) Nd7 8 Ng3 Bg6 9 h4 h5 10 Be2 Qa5 11 b4 Qd5 12 0-0 and Black's Queen is a target in the center and he has a weak Pawn on "h5".

Another very common line for Black is to play 4...Bf5 developing and attacking White's Knight on "e4". A possible continuation is 5 Ng3 Bg6 6 h4 h6 7 Nf3 Nd7 8 h5 Bh7 9 Bd3 Bxd3 10 Qxd3 e6 11 Bd2 Qc7 12 0-0-0 Ngf6 13 Ne4 0-0-0 14 g3 Nxe4 (or if 14...Nc5 15 Nxc5 Bxc5 16 c4 Rhe8 17 Bc3) 15 Qxe4 Nf6 16 Qe2 Bd6 17 c4 c5 18 Bc3 and White is slightly better.

5 Bc4

White actively develops his Bishop, attacking Black's weak Pawn on "f7". Other reasonable book lines which give White a small spatial advantage are 5 Nf3 Ngf6

6 Nxf6+ Nxf6 7 Ne5 Nd7 8 Nd3, or 5 Ng5 Ngf6 6 Bd3 e6 7 N1f3 Bd6 8 Qe2 h6 9 Ne4 Nxe4 10 Qxe4 Nf6 (if 10...Qc7 then 11 Qg4 attacking the "g" Pawn is strong) 11 Qe2 Qc7 12 Bd2 b6 13 0-0-0 Bb7 14 Ne5.

White could have set up a well-known trap with 5 Qe2?. This is actually weak because it blocks the Bishop on "f1". However, White hopes that Black doesn't see the smothered mate and continues blindly with 5...Ngf6?? 6 Nd6++. Black could have simply played 5...e6 or 5...Ndf6.

5...Ngf6

Black develops his Knight toward the center threatening White's Knight on "e4".

6 Ng5

Diagram 140. Position after 6 Ng5

White gets his Knight out of attack with the threat of 7 Bxf7++.

6...Nd5

Black blocks White's Bishop, which threatened 7 Bf7++. However, stronger here is the usual book move 6...e6 freeing the Bishop on "f8" and avoiding moving the same piece twice. After 6...e6 the line might continue 7 Qe2 (threatening 8 Nxf7) Nb6 8 Bd3 (also playable is 8 Bb3, which might continue 8...h6 9 N5f3 a5 10 a3 a4 11 Ba2 c5 12 Bf4 Nbd5 13 Be5) h6 9 N5f3 c5 10 dxc5 Bxc5 11 Ne5 Nbd7 12 Ngf3 Nxe5 13 Nxe5 0-0 and White has the choice of maintaining a slight edge with 14 0-0 b6 15 Rd1 Qe7 16 Bf4 Bb7 17 c3 Rfd8 18 Bg3 or playing a very complicated gambit line with 14 Bd2 Qd5 15 0-0-0 Qxa2 16 c3.

7 N1f3

White develops his Knight toward the center and opens up the possibility of castling.

7...h6

Black attacks and drives White's Knight away from its aggressive post. Though this drives the Knight to a central square, Black plans to develop with an attack on the Knight.

8 Ne4

White gets his Knight out of attack, moving it to an active central square.

8...N7b6

Black attacks White's Bishop while opening up the "h3-c8" diagonal for his Bishop. Another reasonable move was 8...N7f6. However, after 9 Nxf6+ if Black avoids getting doubled Pawns by playing 9...Nxf6 White gets a good game after 10 Ne5 e6 11 0-0.

9 Bb3

Diagram 141. Position after 9 Bb3

White gets his Bishop out of attack while maintaining it on the long "a2-g8" diagonal.

9...Bf5

Black develops a Bishop to an active post where it attacks White's centrally located Knight.

10 Qe2

White brings his Queen to a more active post where she defends the Knight. However, getting the Knight out of attack and attacking Black's Bishop with 10 Ng3 was a good alternative.

10...e6

This frees the Bishop on "f8" and adds to Black's coverage in the center.

11 0-0

White gets his King out of the center and into safety while activating his Rook.

11...Qc7

Black brings his Queen to a more active post while preparing to castle Queenside.

12 Ne5

Diagram 142. Position after 12 Ne5

White places his Knight on its most natural outpost.

12...Bxe4

Black attempts to simplify the game with an exchange. However, this has the drawback of giving White the Bishop pair. If Black tried attacking White's actively posted Knight on "e5" with 12...Nd7 then White could have reinforced his Knight and gained a great position with 13 f4. If Black tried driving away White's actively posted Knight with 12...f6 White could take advantage of the weakened "h5-e8" diagonal with 13 Qh5+ g6 14 Nxg6 Qf7 15 Nxf6+ Nxf6 16 Qxf5 exf5 17 Bxf7+ Kxf7 18 Nxh8+ Kg7 19 Bxh6+ Kxh6 20 Nf7+.

13 Qxe4

White recovers his piece.

13...Nf6

Black repositions his Knight while attacking White's Queen. However, this does not improve the location of Black's Knight, nor does it drive the Queen to an inferior post. Black would have done better to play 13...Nd7, though White would have a nice advantage after 14 f4.

14 Qe2

White gets his Queen out of attack while placing her on a flexible and active post. On "e2" she keeps the pressure on the half-open "e" file, reinforces the Knight on "e5", covers the 2nd rank, and covers two nice diagonals.

14...0-0-0??

Diagram 143. Position after 14...0-0-0

Black intended to get his King out of the center and threaten White's "d" Pawn. However Black's last move was a fatal mistake. Black should have prepared to castle Kingside and develop with 14...Bd6.

See if you can find White's best move here without looking at the next move in the game.

15 Nxf7!

This is the move that Black completely overlooked. It shows that Masters can blunder like anyone else!

White's Knight is forking Black's Rooks. Black cannot play 15...Qxf7 because of 16 Be6+ forking Black's King and Queen! Black resigned here.

l e s s o n

14

Killer Pins

Alexander Alekhine versus Aron Nimzowitsch
San Remo, 1930

Opening: French Defense

Alexander Alekhine was the World Champion from 1927–1935 and then again from 1937 until his death in 1946. Born in Moscow, Russia in 1892, Alekhine was a true chess fanatic who looked at chess as a serious art.

Aron Nimzowitsch was born in Riga, Latvia, in 1886. He is best known for developing positional theories, which he put in his famous book, *My System*. He was known to be a very temperamental and conceited player who had moderately good successes in tournament play.

This game has several very instructive elements. The effective use of Pawns to gain space in the center and on the Queenside is demonstrated. After gaining his spatial advantage White then gets a killer pin on Black's Knight on both a diagonal and an open file. White positions his Rooks and Queen on the open file using the principle of piling up on a pinned piece. And to finish Black off White runs Black out of moves, putting him into zugzwang with most of the pieces on the board!

137

1 e4 e6

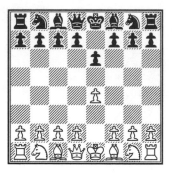

Diagram 144. Position after 1...e6

This is known as the French Defense. With "e6" Black prepares support for the "d" Pawn to counter in the center with 2...d5. Though the idea of supporting "d5" is similar to the Caro-Kann Defense, this game takes on very different characteristics. A main drawback of the French Defense is that the Pawn on "e6" blocks the development of Black's Bishop on "c8". This Bishop is often called "the bad Bishop", or "problem child" of the French Defense. We will get to the strong points of the French Defense soon.

2 d4

White occupies the center with a second Pawn and helps to free up his Queenside pieces.

2...d5

Black occupies the center himself with a Pawn and threatens White's Pawn on "e4".

3 Nc3

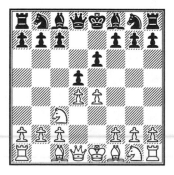

Diagram 145. Position after 3 Nc3

White develops his Knight toward the center and defends his "e" Pawn. Now for an overview of some other options for White.

White could have avoided a pin on his Knight by playing the Tarrasch Variation with 3 Nd2. This has the drawback of temporarily blocking White's Bishop on "c1". After 3 Nd2 the game might continue 3...c5 (also possible is 3...Nf6 4 e5 Nfd7 5 Bd3 c5 6 c3 Nc6) 4 Ngf3 cxd4 5 Nxd4 (also possible is 5 exd5 Qxd5 6 Bc4 Qd6 7 0-0 Nf6 8 Nb3 Nc6 9 Nbxd4) Nf6 6 e5 Nfd7 7 N2f3 Nc6 8 Nxc6 bxc6 9 Bd3.

Another possibility for White is the Advance Variation with 3 e5. After 3 e5 Black will begin to attack White's Pawn chain with 3...c5 and the game might continue 4 c3 Nc6 5 Nf3 Qb6 (also possible is 5...Bd7 6 Be2 Nge7 7 0-0 Ng6 8 Be3) 6 a3 Bd7 7 b4 cxd4 8 cxd4 Rc8 9 Be3.

3...Bb4

This is known as the Winawer Variation. Black immediately develops his Bishop thereby pinning White's Knight and threatening White's "e" Pawn again.

Another common move here for Black was to play 3...Nf6, developing and threatening White's "e" Pawn. After 3...Nf6 the game might continue 4 Bg5 Be7 (other possibilities are 4...dxe4 5 Nxe4 Be7 6 Bxf6 Bxf6 7 Nf3 0-0 8 Qd2 Nd7 9 0-0-0, or 4...Bb4 5 e5 h6 6 Bd2 Bxc3 7 bxc3 Ne4 8 Qg4 g6 9 Qf4 c5 10 Bd3 Nxd2 11 Qxd2 Nc6 12 Nf3 Qa5 13 dxc5 Qxc5 14 0-0 Bd7 15 Rab1) 5 e5 Nfd7 6 Bxe7 Qxe7 7 f4 0-0 (not 7...c5? because of 8 Nb5, or if 7...a6 then 8 Qg4 is strong) 8 Nf3 c5 9 dxc5 Nc6 10 Bd3 f5 (not 10...Qxc5? because White has the Classic Bishop Sacrifice with 11 Bxh7+ Kxh7 12 Ng5+ Kg6 13 Qd3+ f5 14 exf6+ Kxf6 15 Nce4+ winning Black's Queen, or if 12...Kg8 then 13 Qh5 wins) 11 exf6 Qxf6 12 g3 Nxc5 13 0-0 Bd7 14 Qd2 Nxd3 15 cxd3 Be8 16 Rae1 Bg6 17 Ne5 Nxe5 18 Rxe5 Bf5 19 Qe3.

4 e5

White gets his Pawn out of attack and prevents Black from developing his Knight to "f6".

4...c5

This is Black's thematic move in the French Defense. Black attacks the base of White's Pawn chain in an attempt to undermine it. Whereas White hopes his Pawn on "e5" will cramp Black, Black hopes to make White's "e" Pawn into a target. Another part of Black's plan may consist of further nibbling away at White's Pawn center and opening up the "f" file with "f6".

5 Bd2

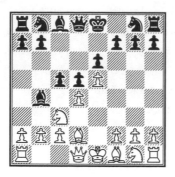

Diagram 146. Position after 5 Bd2

Not the most common move here, but an excellent idea. White totally ignores Black's threat on his "d" Pawn so he can develop a piece and break the pin on the Knight. This gives the Knight the possibility of heading to "b5" where it will attack Black's weak "d6" square.

By far the most common book move here is to immediately attack White's Bishop with 5 a3. After 5 a3 the game might continue 5...Bxc3+ 6 bxc3 Ne7 7 Qg4 0-0 8 Bd3 Nbc6 9 Nf3 f5 10 exf6 Rxf6 with a lively game.

5...Ne7

Black develops a Knight and prepares to castle. More often than not the unprepared player will go Pawn grabbing with 5...cxd4. This allows White to take advantage of Black's weakness on "d6" with 6 Nb5 Bxd2+ (if 6...Bc5 then 7 Qg4 is strong, or if 6...Bf8 then 7 Nf3 Nc6 8 Nbxd4 Qb6 9 Bc3) 7 Qxd2 Nc6 8 f4 Nge7 9 Nd6+ Kf8 10 Nf3 Qb6 11 0-0-0.

6 Nb5

This is White's most aggressive line here. White attacks Black's weak "d6" square with a discovered attack on Black's Bishop on "b4". A good alternative for White was 6 a3 Bxc3 7 Bxc3 Nbc6 (if 7...cxd4 8 Qxd4 Nbc6 9 Qg4, or if 7...b6 8 Qg4 0-0 9 Nf3 Ba6 10 Bxa6 Nxa6 11 0-0) 8 Nf3 cxd4 9 Nxd4 Nxe5 (if 9...0-0 then 10 f4 gives White a good game) 10 Nxe6 Bxe6 11 Bxe5 0-0 12 Bd3 Nc6 13 Bg3.

6...Bxd2+

Black exchanges his Bishop to avoid getting doubled Pawns. If Black played 6...0-0 then White would get a good game after 7 Bxb4 cxb4 8 Bd3.

7 Qxd2

White recovers his piece.

7...0-0

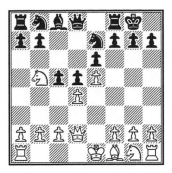

Diagram 147. Position after 7...0-0

Black gets his King out of the center before White has a chance to play Nd6+.

8 c3

White reinforces his "d" Pawn and creates a long Pawn chain. Another reasonable line here was 8 dxc5 Nd7 9 Qc3 Nc6 10 Nf3 b6 11 cxb6 Qxb6 12 a4.

8...b6

Black's idea is to develop his "bad" Bishop to "a6" and exchange it for White's superior Bishop on "f1". A reasonable alternative was the direct developing move 8...Nc6.

9 f4

White reinforces his Pawn on "e5" and builds a massive Pawn center.

9...Ba6

Black continues with his plan of developing and exchanging his "bad" Bishop.

10 Nf3

White develops his Knight, reinforcing his Pawn center.

10...Qd7

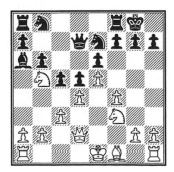

Diagram 148. Position after 10...Qd7

Black brings his Queen to a more active post, attacking White's Knight on "b5" a second time.

11 a4

White defends his threatened Knight on "b5".

11...Nbc6

Black develops his Knight toward the center with the possibility of attacking White's weak "b3" square with 12...Na5. To be considered was 11...Bxb5 exchanging his "bad" Bishop for White's actively posted Knight.

See if you can find White's best move here without looking at the next move in the game.

12 b4!

White takes the initiative on the Queenside and prevents Black's Knight from going to "a5".

12...cxb4

Black relieves the pressure on "c5". If Black played 12...c4 White would have played 13 Nd6 threatening a fork with 14 b5. White would have then had excellent attacking chances on the Kingside.

13 cxb4

Diagram 149. Position after 13 cxb4

White recovers his Pawn.

13...Bb7

Black retreats his Bishop due to fears of a possible Pawn fork on "b5" and discovered attack by White's Bishop. The retreat will also open up the possibility for Black to counter with "a5". To be considered was the more aggressive 13...Nf5.

14 Nd6

White sinks his Knight deep into enemy territory and opens up the "f1-a6" diagonal for his Bishop. The Knight on "d6" greatly restricts the mobility of Black's pieces.

14...f5?

Black stops the advance of White's Pawns on the Kingside. However, Black's real problems are on the Queenside. Black should have countered with 14...a5 planning to meet 15 b5 with 15...Nb4, or challenge White's actively posted Knight on "d6" with 14...Nc8.

15 a5

Diagram 150. Position after 15 a5

White continues with the advance of his Pawns on the Queenside.

15...Nc8

Black seeks to challenge and eliminate White's actively posted Knight on "d6". However, this will bring Black little relief. If 15...bxa5, then White would have played 16 b5 driving Black's Knight back.

16 Nxb7

White exchanges his Knight, which was attacked twice. Now that Black has white-square weaknesses on the Queenside, it is to White's advantage to eliminate Black's Bishop.

16...Qxb7

Black recovers the piece.

17 a6

White drives away Black's Queen from defending on the Queenside while closing off any opportunities for Black to seek counterplay on that flank. White can then focus on taking advantage of the open "c" file.

17...Qf7

Black tries to get his Queen to a square where she will not become a target again. If Black played 17...Qe7 White would play 18 Bb5! as Black's Knight would become trapped if he played 18...Nxb4.

18 Bb5

Diagram 151. Position after 18 Bb5

White begins his build-up on Black's Knight on "c6". White will soon increase this pressure by utilizing the open "c" file with his Rooks and Queen. There is nothing Black can do long-term to prevent Black's eventual breakthrough.

18...N8e7

Black defends his Knight on "c6" and opens up "c8" for use by a Rook. Black will try to make a stand on "c6" in an effort to prevent White from penetrating on the "c" file.

19 0-0

Since White's King was in no danger, the main reason for castling was to bring a second Rook into play to be used on the open "c" file.

19...h6

Although 20 Ng5 was not an immediate threat, Black makes sure it doesn't become one. Since space and not time is Black's problem, the time taken to play 19...h6 will not make a difference.

20 Rfc1

White begins his build-up on the open "c" file and threatens Black's Knight on "c6".

20...Rfc8

Black defends his Knight on "c6" which was threatened. Retreating the Knight to "b8" or "d8" would allow devastating penetration with 21 Rc7.

21 Rc2

Diagram 152. Position after 21 Rc2

White prepares to double his Rooks by opening up "c1" for the other Rook.

21...Qe8

Black submits himself to a pin along the "a4-e8" diagonal in order to add protection to his Knight on "c6". This may seem foolish, but there is no solution to Black's problems. If Black played 21...Nd8 White would be able to penetrate on the "c" file after 22 Rac1 Rxc2 23 Rxc2 Rc8 (or if 23...Ng6 then 24 Qc1) 24 Rxc8 Nxc8 25 Qc2 Ne7 26 Qc7.

22 Rac1

White continues with his plan of doubling his Rooks on the open "c" file. However, White had a more direct way of finishing Black off. He could have played 22 Qc1with the idea of tripling on the "c" file with 23 Ra3 and 24 Rac3.

22...Rab8

Black's idea here is to meet 23 Ba4 with 23...b5.

23 Qe3

If given the opportunity White's plan is to play 24 Qa3 followed by 25 Qa4, furthering the attack on Black's Knight on "c6".

23...Rc7

Black responds by preparing to double his Rooks on the "c" file to aid in the defense of his Knight on "c6".

24 Rc3

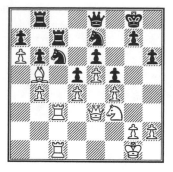

Diagram 153. Position after 24 Rc3

White finally sees the light. His plan consists of clearing the "c1" square for his Queen so that he can triple on the open "c" file.

24...Qd7

Black clears the "e8" square so that his King can be maneuvered to the Queenside. Black will defend his Rook on "c7" with his King in an attempt to defend against the pin along the "c" file.

25 R1c2

White opens up the "c1" square for use by his Queen.

25...Kf8

Black begins to move his King to the Queenside to help with the defense.

26 Qc1

White completes tripling on the open "c" file, attacking Black's Knight on "c6" a fourth time. Black must now defend his Knight with a fourth piece to avoid losing it. As a general rule, *"When tripling with two Rooks and a Queen along an open file it is best to place the Queen at the rear."*

26...Rbc8

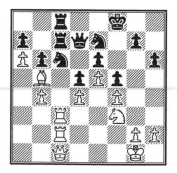

Diagram 154. Position after 26...Rbc8

Black defends his Knight on "c6" with a fourth piece to avoid its immediate loss. See if you can find White's best move here without looking at the next move in the game.

27 Ba4

White clears the "b5" square for use by his Pawn. White's idea is to use his "b" Pawn to attack and win Black's pinned Knight on "c6".

27...b5

Black sacrifices a Pawn to delay the loss of his Knight on "c6".

28 Bxb5

White wins a Pawn and maintains his second pin on Black's Knight on "c6".

28...Ke8

Diagram 155. Position after 28...Ke8

Black continues with his plan of bringing his King toward the Queenside to help defend.

29 Ba4

White once again opens up "b5" for use by his Pawn.

29...Kd8

Black defends his Rook on "c7" with a third piece in an attempt to defend against the pin on the "c" file.

30 h4

Diagram 156. Position after 31 h4

This is an amazing "zugzwang" position. Any piece that Black moves other than a Pawn will result in the immediate loss of material. For example if Black plays 30...Qe8, then 31 b5. White can simply make waiting moves and run Black out of Pawn moves. Black resigned here.

l e s s o n

15

Sacrificing Against the Castled King

Snyder versus Howeth
Santa Monica, 1971

Opening: Sicilian Defense

This is another game where White builds up on the Kingside and obtains a strong attack against the castled King. First a Knight sacrifice is used to open up the King, followed by a Queen sacrifice to deliver the checkmate.

1 e4 c5

Black initiates the Sicilian Defense. It is one of the most popular openings. Black would like to exchange his flank Pawn (on "c5") for White's center Pawn (on "d4"), obtaining the use of the "c" file and freeing his Queen on the "a5-d8" diagonal. Black often obtains most of the play on the Queenside, White plays on the Kingside and there is a lively fight in the center.

2 f4

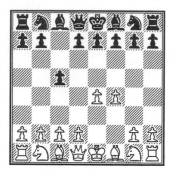

Diagram 157. Position after 2 f4

This is less popular than the usual 2 Nf3, which will be covered in the next lesson. Known as the Grand Prix attack, White immediately indicates his intentions of playing aggressively on the Kingside and in the center. White attacks the important "e5" square and plans, when he castles Kingside, to have his Rook on "f1" actively placed and the "e1-h4" diagonal available for use by his Queen.

2...e6

Besides opening the diagonal for his Bishop on "f8" Black intends to use his "e" Pawn to support "d5". We will take a look at some examples of other possible lines.

One of the most popular and strongest moves is for Black to immediately strike at the center with 2...d5. If 3 exd5 Black can play a strong gambit with 3...Nf6. The game might continue 4 Bb5+ Bd7 5 Bxd7+ Qxd7 6 c4 e6 7 Qe2 Bd6 8 dxe6 fxe6 9 d3 0-0 10 Nf3 Nc6 11 0-0 Rae8 12 Nc3 e5 13 f5 Nd4.

Therefore, after 2...d5 White would be better off not accepting the gambit and considering 3 Nc3 where Black has several reasonable choices. If 3...dxe4, the game might continue 4 Nxe4 e6 5 Nf3 Nc6 6 Bb5 Bd7 7 0-0. If 3...d4, then 4 Nce2 Nc6 5 Nf3 Nf6 6 d3 Bg4 7 Ng3. If 3...e6, then 4 Bb5+ Bd7 5 Bxd7+ Qxd7 6 d3 Nc6 7 Nf3 dxe4 8 Nxe4. And, finally if 3...Nf6, then 4 e5 d4 5 exf6 dxc3 6 fxg7 cxd2+ 7 Qxd2 Qxd2+ 8 Bxd2 Bxg7 9 0-0-0.

Another popular second move for Black is 2...Nc6 and after 3 Nf3 Black has some reasonable choices. If 3...d6, the game might continue 4 Bb5 Bd7 5 Nc3 g6 6 0-0 Bg7 7 d3 Nf6 8 Qe1. If 3...e6, then 4 Nc3 d5 5 Bb5 Nge7 6 exd5 exd5 7 Qe2.

The immediate fianchetto with 2...g6 is often played. The game might continue 3 Nf3 Bg7 4 Nc3 Nc6 5 Bb5 Nd4 6 a4 (6 0-0 is also playable) e6 7 e5 a6 8 Bc4 d5 9 exd6 Qxd6 10 d3 Nf6 11 Ne4 Qc7 12 c3.

3 Nf3

White develops his Knight toward the center.

3...d5

Black continues with his plan of aggressively using his Pawns to attack in the center.

4 Bb5+

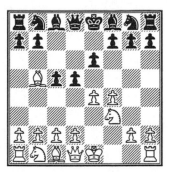

Diagram 158. Position after 4 Bb5+

It is difficult to find a better square for this Bishop. Therefore, White solves this problem by exchanging it and allowing for early Kingside castling. If 4 Nc3, Black gets a comfortable game after 4...dxe4 5 Nxe4 Nf6 6 Bb5+ Bd7 7 Bxd7+ Nbxd7.

4...Bd7

Black parries the check and challenges White's Bishop. Black doesn't mind exchanging his bad Bishop.

5 Bxd7+

White follows through with his plan of exchanging his Bishop. He doesn't want to be burdened by trying to protect it on "b5".

5...Qxd7

Black recovers his Bishop. It is reasonable to recapture with 5...Nxd7 where White does best to reinforce his center with 6 d3. However, in the game the text move keeps Black's option of developing his Knight on "b8" to the more active "c6" square.

6 exd5

Here, I usually recommend to my students 6 Ne5, which may continue 6...Qc7 7 exd5 exd5 8 Nc3 Nf6 (if 8...d4 9 Nb5 Qb6 10 Qg4!) 9 Qf3 Nc6 (if 9...d4 10 Nb5 Qb6 11 Qb3!, or if 9...Qd8 then 10 Qe2!) 10 Nxd5 Nxd5 11 Qxd5 Rd8 12 Qe4 and Black doesn't have enough compensation for his Pawn.

6...Qxd5

Playing 6...exd5 7 Ne5 Qc7 would transpose into the notes to White's 6th move. Since this is unfavorable for Black he decides to recover the Pawn with his Queen.

7 Nc3

Diagram 159. Position after 7 Nc3

White develops his Knight toward the center, gaining time by attacking Black's Queen.

7...Qd8

Black gets his Queen out of attack. She goes to a square where she is least likely to be exposed to attack again and has numerous good squares where she can be repositioned.

8 Ne5

The Knight takes its natural outpost. Black cannot develop his Knight to its most natural post with 8...Nc6 because White would double and isolate Black's Pawns after 9 Nxc6 bxc6. One of the advantages of White's second move (2 f4) has now become more apparent—it helps support the Knight on "e5".

8...Nf6

Black develops his Knight toward the center as part of his preparations to castle Kingside.

9 d3

White frees his Bishop on "c1" while covering the important "e4" and "c4" squares. In most variations of the Grand Prix Attack (1 e4 c5 2 f4) White avoids playing "d4", which would allow Black to exchange his flank Pawn for White's center Pawn. Instead the Pawn on "f4" helps balance the control for the center.

9...Be7

Black develops his Bishop continuing with his preparations to castle.

10 0-0

Diagram 160. Position after 10 0-0

White gets his King out of the center and into safety. Because of the Pawn on "f4" White's Rook on "f1" is more actively posted after castling.

10...0-0

Black gets his King out of the center. It is true that White will build a nice attack on the Kingside, but the options of leaving the King in the center or attempting to castle Queenside were less attractive.

11 Qf3

This continues the Kingside build-up. White's Queen is very well posted on "f3". She threatens Black's Pawn on "b7", covers the Knight when it goes to "e4", has greater access to various attacking posts on the Kingside and is out of the way when White's Rook on "a1" is moved to "e1".

11...Nd5

Black centralizes his Knight and blocks White's Queen's attack on "b7". It would have been reasonable for Black to defend the "b" Pawn with 11...Qc7. White would then continue with a similar plan as used in the game by developing with 12 Bd2, freeing the Rook on "a1" to go to "e1".

12 Bd2

Simple and good! White develops his Bishop and allows his Rook on "a1" to come into play.

12...a6?

It was difficult for Black to find a good move here. However, this move serves little constructive purpose. Playing 12...f6 would weaken the "e" Pawn but at least after 13 Nc4 Black could develop with 13...Nc6 without obtaining doubled isolated Pawns.

13 Rae1

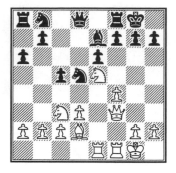

Diagram 161. Position after 13 Rae1

White continues with his build-up. The Rook comes into play along a central file.

13...Bf6

Black brings his Bishop to a more active square where it will help defend on the Kingside and attack in the center.

14 Ne4

White brings his Knight to a central square in theme with his Kingside build-up.

14...Bxe5?

In his attempt to simplify and relieve pressure through exchanges, Black brings White's Pawn to a strong square on "e5" where it attacks the "d6" and "f6" squares and cramps Black's game. Black should have continued developing with 14...Nd7.

15 fxe5

Diagram 162. Position after 15 fxe5

White recovers his piece.

15...Qc7

Black tries to get counterplay by attacking White's unprotected "e" Pawn.

16 Qh5

White defends his "e" Pawn while positioning his Queen on a stronger post where she attacks "f7" and "h7" to aid in the attack.

16...Nc6

Diagram 163. Position after 16...Nc6

Black finally completes his minor piece development. But it does little good against White's attack at this point.

See if you can find White's best move here without looking at the next move in the game.

17 Nf6+!

White sacrifices his Knight to expose Black's King to a powerful attack.

17...gxf6

Black has nothing better to do than to accept the sacrifice. If 17...Nxf6 then 18 exf6 (threatening 19 Qg5 g6 20 Qh6 followed by mate on "g7") gxf6 19 Re4 Rfd8 20 Bh6 Kh8 21 Rh4 Rd5 22 Bg5 Kg8 23 Qxh7+ Kf8 24 Bxf6 Ke8 25 Qg8+ Kd7 26 Qxa8.

18 exf6

White now threatens 19 Qg5+ Kh8 20 Qg7++.

18...Kh8

Black tries to prepare to defend his "h7" square by placing his Rook on "g8", sacrificing his Knight on "f6" and moving his Rook to "g7". Nice idea, but it doesn't work!

19 Re4

White plans to place his Rook on "h4" setting up a mate on "h7".

19...Rg8

Diagram 164. Position after 19...Rg8

Black plans to meet 20 Rh4 with 20...Nxf6 21 Rxf6 Rg7. However, the game would still have been hopeless after 22 Bh6 Rag8 23 Bxg7+ Rxg7 24 Rh6 f5 25 Qe8+.

See if you can find White's best move here without looking at the next move in the game.

20 Qxh7+!

White sacrifices his Queen to open up Black's King and force a mate in two more moves.

20...Kxh7

Black's only legal move is to accept the sacrifice.

21 Rh4+

White now brings his Rook into the attack on Black's King along the opened "h" file.

21...Kg6

Moving his King out toward his death is Black's only legal move.

22 Rh6++

Diagram 165. Position after 22 Rh6++

Black has been checkmated!

l e s s o n

16

The Final Game

Fischer versus Spassky
Iceland, 1972

Opening: Sicilian Defense

This is the last game of the famous World Championship match where Bobby Fischer defeated Boris Spassky. The game has numerous instructive elements, which include allowing doubled isolated Pawns to obtain a strong Pawn center and Bishop Pair, and an endgame with a minor piece and Pawn versus a Rook.

1 e4 c5 2 Nf3

Diagram 166. Position after 2 Nf3

This is the most common move played here. White develops a Knight toward the center and prepares support for 3 d4.

2...e6

This is one of several common moves played here. Black frees his Bishop on "f8" and covers the important "d5" and "f5" squares. With his Pawn on "e6" Black has increased the likelihood of aggressively attacking in the center with "d5".

The most common move here for Black is 2...d6. After 2...d6 the game might continue, 3 d4 cxd4 4 Nxd4 Nf6 5 Nc3 g6 (or 5...a6 6 Bg5 e6 7 f4, known as the Najdorf Variation) 6 Be3 Bg7 7 f3, known as the Dragon Variation.

3 d4

White boldly strikes at the center attacking Black's "c" Pawn. This move also helps to free White's Queenside pieces.

3...cxd4

Black takes care of the attack on his "c" Pawn by exchanging it for White's center Pawn.

4 Nxd4

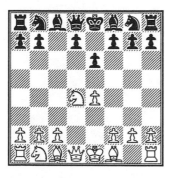

Diagram 167. Position after 4 Nxd4

White recovers his Pawn and centralizes his Knight.

4...a6

This is a very common move in many variations of the Sicilian Defense. Black prevents White from moving a Knight or Bishop to "b5" while preparing to possibly expand on the Queenside by moving his Pawn to "b5". In the Sicilian Defense Black usually gets most of the play on the Queenside, while White is more aggressively situated on the Kingside.

5 Nc3

White develops his Knight toward the center providing protection for his "e" Pawn. Developing his Bishop and defending the "e" Pawn with 5 Bd3 was also possible. This would have allowed White the possibility of getting in "c4" to increase his foothold on the "d5" square. After 5 Bd3 the game might have continued 5...Nf6 6 0-0 d6 7 c4 Be7 8 Nc3 0-0 9 Be3.

5...Nc6

Black develops his Knight, challenging White's centralized Knight in the center.

6 Be3

White develops his Bishop to an active square and adds protection to his Knight on "d4". It would have also been good to develop the other Bishop and prepare for castling with 6 Be2. After 6 Be2 the game might have continued 6...Qc7 7 0-0 Nf6 8 Be3 Bb4 9 Na4 (attacking Black's weak "b6" square and preventing Black from playing 9...Bxc3) and now not 9...Nxe4? because of 10 Nxc6 Qxc6 11 Nb6 Rb8 12 Qd4 Bf8 13 Bf3 and White has more than enough compensation for the sacrificed Pawn.

6...Nf6

Black develops his Knight toward the center putting pressure on White's "e" Pawn and preparing support for a possible future "d5". A reasonable alternative was to post the Queen actively with 6...Qc7. The game might have continued 7 Bd3 Nf6 8 0-0 Ne5 9 h3 Bc5 10 Qe2 d6 11 f4.

7 Bd3

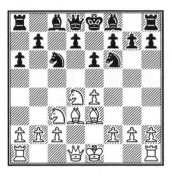

Diagram 168. Position after 7 Bd3

White completes his minor piece development and prepares to castle.

7...d5

Black boldly attacks in the center. He is willing to accept an isolated Pawn to gain more space in the center and free his Bishop on "c8". Bringing the Queen into play with 7...Qc7 was also playable.

8 exd5

White eliminates the pressure on his "e" Pawn and gives Black an isolated Pawn.

8...exd5

Black recovers his Pawn and frees his Bishop on "c8". White would have obtained a nice advantage after 8...Nxd5 9 Nxc6 bxc6 10 Nxd5 cxd5 11 Bd4.

9 0-0

White removes his King from the center while bringing his Rook to a more active location. A reasonable alternative for White was 9 Qd2 with the option of castling Queenside.

9...Bd6

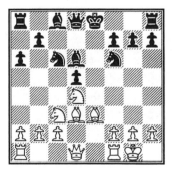

Diagram 169. Position after 9...Bd6

Black develops his Bishop to the long "h2-b8" diagonal while preparing to castle Kingside. White's pieces are not effectively placed to take advantage of Black's isolated "d" Pawn.

10 Nxc6?

This only strengthens Black's Pawn center. White's plan is to open up his "d4" square to centralize his Bishop. A stronger move for White here was 10 h3 preventing Black's Knight from going to "g4".

10...bxc6

Black recovers his Knight.

11 Bd4

White centralizes his Bishop and puts pressure on Black's Knight on "f6".

11...0-0

Black gets his King out of the center and off the open "e" file.

12 Qf3

Diagram 170. Position after 12 Qf3

White brings his Queen into play and attacks Black's Knight on "f6" a second time. Also playable was 12 h3 preventing Black's Knight from going to "g4".

12...Be6

Black completes his minor piece development. This move adds protection to Black's "d" Pawn, which frees the "c" Pawn to advance. Black avoided falling for a trap with 12...Bg4??, which would lose a piece after 13 Bxf6.

An interesting alternative for Black was 12...Ng4, threatening White's "h" Pawn and freeing his Queen on the "h4-d8" diagonal. The game might have continued 13 h3 Qh4 (not 13...Nh2? because of 14 Qh5) 14 Rfe1 Nh2 (or if 14...c5 the game might have continued 15 Bxc5 Bxc5 16 hxg4 Bxg4 17 Qf4 Rfd8 18 g3 Qh5 19 Re5 f5

20 Be2 Bxe2 21 Nxe2 with about even chances) 15 Qe3 Bxh3 16 Be5 (if 16 gxh3 then 16...Qxd4 17 Qxd4 Nf3+ 18 Kg2 Nxd4 and Black is a Pawn ahead) d4! 17 Qe4! (if 17 Bxd4 then 17...Bxg2 18 Kxg2 Qg4+ 19 Kh1 Nf3, or if 17 Qxd4 then 17...Nf3+! 18 gxf3 Qg5+ 19 Bg3 Bxg3 20 Kh1 Be5) Qxe4 18 Rxe4 Bxe5 19 Rxe5 dxc3 20 Kxh2 cxb2 21 Rab1 Be6 22 Rxb2 and though Black is a Pawn ahead White's active pieces will even up the score.

13 Rfe1

White brings his Rook into play on the open "e" file.

13...c5!

Black mobilizes his center Pawns, driving White's Bishop from its active post on "d4". Black allows White to give him doubled isolated Pawns. In return Black will have active Pawns in the center and the Bishop pair.

14 Bxf6

White exchanges his Bishop, which must leave its central post. If 14 Be5, Black is clearly better after 14...Bxe5 15 Rxe5 Qd6.

14...Qxf6

Black recovers his piece. Black would certainly not play 14...gxf6?, because of 15 Qh5.

15 Qxf6

White continues with his plan of giving Black doubled isolated Pawns.

15...gxf6

Diagram 171. Position after 15...gxf6

Black recovers his Queen.

16 Rad1

White brings a second Rook onto a central file which will help combat Black's active Pawn center.

16...Rfd8

Black counters by also placing a Rook on the "d" file. This helps support his "d" Pawn.

17 Be2

White opens up the "d" file for his Rook to apply pressure on Black's "d" Pawn. This also allows for the possibility of attacking the "d" Pawn again by posting the Bishop on "f3".

17...Rab8

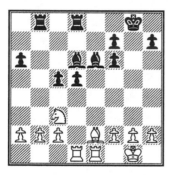

Diagram 172. Position after 17...Rab8

Black brings his other Rook into play by placing it on a half open file and threatening White's "b" Pawn.

18 b3

White defends his "b" Pawn. White avoids falling for a trap after 18 Nxd5? Bxd5 19 Rxd5 Bxh2+ 20 Kxh2 Rxd5. Also, 18 Bxa6 would allow Black's Rook to penetrate with 18...Rxb2.

18...c4

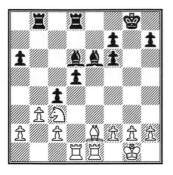

Diagram 173. Position after 18...c4

Black plays aggressively by not allowing White time to consolidate and apply further pressure on the "d" Pawn. Black's immediate threat is 19...Bb4. However, a reasonable alternative, avoiding White's next move, was 18...Be5 19 Na4 c4.

At this point White comes up with an interesting resource. See if you can find White's best move here without looking at the next move in the game.

19 Nxd5!

White will get a Bishop and Pawn with this exchange sacrifice. This should have been good enough to obtain a draw in what would have otherwise been an inferior game for White. Black would have stood better after 19 Na4 Bb4 20 c3 Bf8 21 b4 d4.

19...Bxd5

Black forces White's Rook to recapture on "d5" to set up the discovered attack.

20 Rxd5

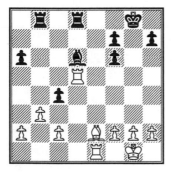

Diagram 174. Position after 20 Rxd5

White recovers his minor piece.

20...Bxh2+

Black uses a discovered attack to win the exchange, uncovering his Rook on White's unprotected Rook on "d5".

21 Kxh2

White captures Black's Bishop.

21...Rxd5

Black captures White's Rook.

22 Bxc4

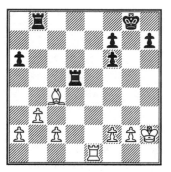

Diagram 175. Position after 22 Bxc4

White has obtained a Bishop and Pawn for his Rook. Because Black has doubled isolated Pawns, in effect White almost has two Pawns for the exchange. Though White may be slightly preferred here, with correct play the game should be a draw. White's plan will be to advance his Pawns on the Queenside. Black's plan will be to somehow utilize his extra doubled Pawn on the Kingside while restraining White's Queenside Pawn advance. Both sides will try to get their Kings into play.

22...Rd2

Black gets his Rook out of attack while attacking White's unprotected "c" and "f" Pawns.

23 Bxa6

White eliminates Black's "a" Pawn, thereby obtaining two connected passed Pawns on the Queenside. White would have done better to play 23 Re2 Rxe2 24 Bxe2. The idea is to keep more Pawns on the board, which decreases the chances of a draw. In this game Spassky needed a win to avoid losing the match and his World Championship title.

23...Rxc2

Black must prevent White from keeping his three connected passed Queenside Pawns. Black now threatens White's "a" and "f" Pawns.

24 Re2

White neutralizes Black's menacing Rook by challenging it.

24...Rxe2

White gets rid of the threat on his Rook by exchanging it for Black's Rook. If 24...Rbc8 White would hold with 25 a4!

25 Bxe2

Diagram 176. Position after 25 Bxe2

White recovers his Rook.

25...Rd8

Black prepares once again to post a Rook actively on his 7th rank.

26 a4

White removes his "a" Pawn from being a target to Black's Rook once it gets to "d2". White also wants to advance his Queenside Pawns, which can pose a serious threat to Black.

26...Rd2

Black actively posts his Rook where it attacks White's Bishop and can get behind White's passed Pawns. As a general rule, *"In the endgame Rooks belong behind passed Pawns."*

27 Bc4

White gets his Bishop out of attack, posting it where it is defended by a Pawn and not blocking the advance of his two passed Pawns.

27...Ra2

Black restrains White's "a" Pawn from advancing by placing his Rook behind it. The game would have been a draw after 27...Rxf2 28 a5 Kf8 29 a6 Rb2 30 Bd5 Ra2 31 Bc4.

28 Kg3

Diagram 177. Position after 28 Kg3

White naturally brings his King into play. As a general rule, *"The King should be used as an active fighting piece in the endgame."* I often tell my students, *"The King is like a vampire, he needs to hide and be protected by day (the opening/middlegame), but at night (the endgame) he becomes powerful, grows fangs and wings and comes out!"*

28...Kf8

And naturally Black begins to bring his King into play.

29 Kf3

It would have been more accurate to play 29 f4. This would make it so that White's King would not have to defend the "f" Pawn. His Bishop ideally would be able to defend the "g" Pawn from "d5". This would help free up White's King from the burden of defending the Kingside Pawns.

29...Ke7

Black continues to bring his King into play.

30 g4?

Diagram 178. Position after 30 g4

This allows Black to obtain an outside passed Pawn. White could have drawn easily with 30 Kg3. See if you can find Black's best move here without looking at the next move in the game.

30...f5!

Black sacrifices a Pawn so that his "h" Pawn becomes an outside Passed Pawn.

31 gxf5

White has nothing better than to accept the Pawn sacrifice since his "g" Pawn was attacked. If White tried to avoid removing his Pawn from the "g" file with 31 g5 then Black would have forced the issue with 31...f6.

31...f6

This frees Black's King from having to defend his "f" Pawn.

32 Bg8

White attacks Black's "h" Pawn.

32...h6

Black gets his "h" Pawn out of attack.

33 Kg3

Diagram 179. Position after 33 Kg3

White keeps his King in a position where it can best restrain a future advance of Black's "h" Pawn.

33...Kd6

Black continues to bring his King into play.

34 Kf3?

The King goes right back where it just came from. White would have offered more resistance by keeping Black's King out of "e5" by playing 34 f4.

34...Ra1

This threatens to place the Rook on "g1", with the idea of cutting off Black's King from interfering with the advance of the "h" Pawn.

35 Kg2

White prevents White's Rook from getting to "g1", which would cut off the King from stopping the advance of the "h" Pawn.

35...Ke5

Black continues to bring his King into play and threatens White's Pawn on "f5".

36 Be6

Diagram 180. Position after 36 Be6

White defends his "f5" Pawn.

36...Kf4

Black has obtained an ideal position for his King. White's Bishop is tied down to the defense of his Pawn on "f5" and Black's King is set up to be able to help support the advance of his "h" Pawn.

37 Bd7

White defends his "a" Pawn, which gives him the possibility of advancing his "b" Pawn.

37...Rb1

Black prevents White's "b" Pawn from advancing while threatening it.

38 Be6

White has no choice but to defend his "b" Pawn.

38...Rb2

Black is tying down White's pieces to the defense of his Pawns.

39 Bc4

Diagram 181. Position after 39 Bc4

White is willing to give up his Pawn on "f5" so that his "a" Pawn can advance. The Bishop on "c4" would be able to support a Pawn on "a6".

39...Ra2

Black now restrains White's "a" Pawn from advancing with the threat of 40...Kxf5.

40 Be6

White defends his Pawn on "f5".

40...h5

Diagram 182. Position after 40...h5

The advance of Black's passed Pawn signaled the end of the game for White. Here the game was adjourned. Spassky's sealed move was 41 Bd7. After careful analysis Spassky realized he was lost and resigned.

After 41 Bd7 Black would win with 41...Kg4 42 b4 (or if 42 Bc6 then 42...h4 43 Bf3+ Kxf5) h4 43 a5 h3+ 44 Kg1 Ra1+ 45 Kh2 Rf1 and White's King is trapped in a mating net.

White's best attempt to defend would have been 41 Kh3. However, Black would still have won after 41...Rxf2 42 a5 h4! 43 a6 Kg5 44 b4 (or if 44 Bd5 then 44...Ra2 45 Bc4 Ra3) Rf3+ 45 Kh2 Kg4 46 Bc4 Rh3+ 47 Kg2 Rg3+ 48 Kh2 h3 49 Be2+ Kh4 50 Bf1 Ra3 51 Bc4 Ra1 52 b5 Rd1 53 a7 Rd2+ 54 Kh1 Kg3 and White cannot prevent mate.

The Wrong Rook

R. Byrne versus Fischer
US Championship, 1963

Opening: Gruenfeld Defense

Often a player is faced with a choice of which Rook to use when they can both go to the same square. And in this game, choosing the wrong Rook was a fatal mistake. This brilliant game contains many instructive elements such as allowing an isolated "d" Pawn in the opening to obtain active piece play, sacrificing against the weakened "f2" square, taking advantage of white square weaknesses and the use of a deep combination.

1 d4

We now start looking at some games using "d" Pawn openings. White places a Pawn in the center freeing his Bishop on "c1", opening "d2" for possible use by a Knight and allowing his Queen to exert pressure in the center. I like to start my beginning students off with "e" Pawn openings. The "e" Pawn openings tend to contain more tactical themes, whereas "d" Pawn openings are usually more positional. Generally beginners understand and relate better to tactics than positional concepts. As a player gets stronger the learning of openings that require an understanding of in-depth positional play is a good idea.

1...Nf6

This is by far the most common opening move here. Black develops a Knight toward the center and prevents White from playing 2 e4.

2 c4

This is White's most common opening move here. White gains more space by continuing to build a Pawn center. As a general rule, *"In 'd' Pawn openings both sides avoid blocking their 'c' Pawns with a Knight."* By moving his "c" Pawn White opens the "d1-a4" diagonal for possible use by his Queen.

2...g6

Diagram 183. Position after 2...g6

Black prepares to fianchetto his Bishop on "g7".

3 g3

White prepares to fianchetto his Bishop on "g2". The most common opening move here is 3 Nc3. This may lead to the King's Indian Defense which might continue 3...Bg7 4 e4 d6 5 Nf3 0-0 6 Be2 e5 7 0-0 Nc6 8 d5 Ne7.

3...c6

Black is in no rush to complete his fianchetto. Black prepares support for his Pawn to go to "d5".

4 Bg2

White completes his fianchetto. An advantage in using a fianchetto is that the Bishop is located on its longest potential diagonal where it is aimed directly at the center. The drawback of preparing a fianchetto is that time must be taken to move a "b" or "g" Pawn. This doesn't attack or occupy the center with a Pawn.

4...d5

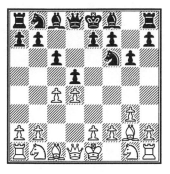

Diagram 184. Position after 4...d5

Black occupies the center with a Pawn, freeing his Queenside pieces and attacking White's unprotected "c" Pawn.

5 cxd5

White eliminates the attack on his "c" Pawn by exchanging it for Black's Pawn.

5...cxd5

Black recovers his Pawn while maintaining a Pawn in the center and opening up "c6" for use by his Knight.

6 Nc3

White develops a Knight toward the center, increasing pressure on Black's "d" Pawn.

6...Bg7

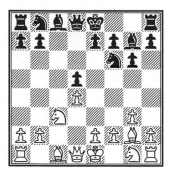

Diagram 185. Position after 6...Bg7

Black completes his fianchetto.

7 e3

White's plan is to develop his Knight to "e2". A drawback of this move is that it leaves White weak on the white squares. A more logical and direct move was 7 Nf3, which may have continued 7...0-0 8 Ne5 with a fairly even game.

7...0-0

Black removes his King from the center.

8 Nge2

White continues with his plan of developing his Knight.

8...Nc6

Black develops his Knight to its most active post.

9 0-0

White removes his King from the center.

9...b6

Diagram 186. Position after 9...b6

Developing the Bishop anywhere along the "h3-c8" diagonal would be awkward since it would either be in the way or a target. Therefore, Black seeks greener pastures for his Bishop by opening up a new diagonal for it. It is not uncommon in "d" Pawn openings that Bishops on "c1" and "c8" are the most difficult minor pieces to develop.

10 b3

White also seeks greener pastures for his Bishop by opening up a new diagonal for it. A reasonable alternative for White would have been to play 10 Nf4 e6 11 Bd2 with an even game.

10...Ba6

Black develops his Bishop to the long "f1-a6" diagonal, pinning White's Knight on "e2".

11 Ba3

White develops his Bishop to the long "a3-f8" diagonal, pinning Black's Pawn on "e7".

11...Re8

Black unpins his "e" Pawn and backs it up with his Rook.

12 Qd2

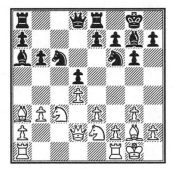

Diagram 187. Position after 12 Qd2

White connects his Rooks and brings his Queen to a more active post. However, 12 Rc1 threatening 13 Nxd5 was stronger.

Up to here the game has been rather quiet. However, Fischer had a rather deep and bold plan in mind. See if you can find Black's best move here without looking at the next move in the game.

12...e5!

The key move! Black doesn't mind getting an isolated "d" Pawn in return for active piece play. This move was risky and required in-depth analysis to be sure it was good.

13 dxe5

White eliminates Black's aggressive Pawn. If White plays passively with 13 Rac1, Black is clearly better after 13...exd4 14 exd4 Rc8.

13...Nxe5

Black recovers his Pawn and posts his Knight actively in the center where it attacks White's weak white squares.

Diagram 188. Position after 13...Nxe5

14 Rfd1?

On the surface it looks like this is the correct Rook to move to "d1". White would ideally like to have his Rooks on both the open "c" and "d" files. However, Fischer will nicely demonstrate that White has no time to execute this plan. White is too weak on the white squares and has now created an additional weakness on "f2".

It would have been better to play 14 Rad1. However, Black comes out on top after 14...Qc8!. If White goes Pawn grabbing with 15 Nxd5, the game might continue, Nxd5 16 Bxd5 Rd8 17 f4 Rxd5 18 Qxd5 Bb7 19 Qd2 (if 19 Qd8+ then 19...Qxd8 20 Rxd8+ Rxd8 21 fxe5 Rd2 22 Rf2 Bxe5 and Black's Bishop pair, better Pawn structure and actively posted Rook give him a major advantage) Qc6 (not 19...Qh3?, because after 20 Nd4 Ng4 21 Nf3 it is White who comes out on top) 20 Qd5 Qxd5 21 Rxd5 Bxd5 22 fxe5 Bxe5 and Black has the Bishop pair and better Pawn structure.

See if you can find Black's best move here without looking at the next move in the game.

14...Nd3!

Black takes advantage of White's weak "d3" square. The Knight blocks White's use of the "d" file, attacks White's weak "f2" square and will be like a thorn in a lion's paw unless White does something to dislodge it. Black is now threatening to bring his other Knight strongly into play and open up the "a1-h8" diagonal for his Bishop with 15...Ne4.

15 Qc2

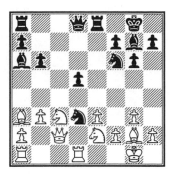

Diagram 189. Position after 15 Qc2

White dislodges Black's Knight by threatening 16 Rxd3. White most certainly anticipated Black's next move, but greatly underestimated its crushing effect!

In light of what happened after the text move, White should have considered keeping Black's Knight from immediately going to "e4" by playing the ugly looking 15 f3. This move may weaken the "e" Pawn and block White's fianchettoed Bishop but would have prevented Black's next move and therefore been the lesser of the evils. The game may have continued with 15...Bh6 16 f4 (if 16 Nf4 then 16...d4 is strong) Bg7 17 Nc1 Ne4 18 Nxe4 dxe4 (not 18...Bxa1 because of 19 Nd6) 19 Rb1 Rc8 with a substantial advantage for Black. Another try would have been 15 Nc1 but once again Black is much better after 15...Ne4 16 Nxe4 dxe4 17 Rb1 Rc8.

See if you can find Black's best move here without looking at the next move in the game.

15...Nxf2!

This is the key move, which cracks open the position and exposes White's King to attack.

16 Kxf2

White has little choice but to accept the sacrifice or otherwise face immediate material loss along with the bad position.

16...Ng4+

Black continues his attack against White's King while also attacking the "e" Pawn and opening the "a1-h8" diagonal for his Bishop.

17 Kg1

White does his best to try to hide his King.

17...Nxe3

Black gets a second Pawn for his sacrificed Knight while attacking White's Queen, Rook and Bishop.

18 Qd2

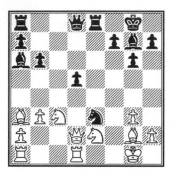

Diagram 190. Position after 18 Qd2

Naturally, White gets his Queen out of attack. See if you can find Black's best move here without looking at the next move in the game.

18...Nxg2!!

Trying to immediately recover material with 18...Nxd1 gives White the advantage after 19 Rxd1. Instead Black removes White's Bishop, leaving his King hopelessly exposed on the white squares.

19 Kxg2

White recovers his minor piece. See if you can find Black's best move here without looking at the next move in the game.

19...d4!

Black sacrifices a Pawn to open up the "h1-a8" diagonal for his Bishop to join the attack on White's exposed King.

20 Nxd4

White had little choice but to eliminate Black's menacing Pawn, which threatened the Knight on "c3".

20...Bb7+

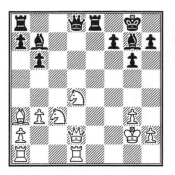

Diagram 191. Position after 20...Bb7+

Black brings his Bishop into the attack against White's King. Here White is lost in all variations.

21 Kf1

White gets his King out of attack. White had his choice of poison. If 21 Kg1, then 21...Bxd4+ 22 Qxd4 Re1+! 23 Kf2 Qxd4+ 24 Rxd4 Rxa1 25 Rd7 Rc8 wins easily. Or if 21 Kf2, then 21...Qd7! 22 Rac1 Qh3 23 Nf3 Bh6 24 Qd3 Be3+ 25 Qxe3 Rxe3 26 Kxe3 Re8+ 27 Kf2 Qf5 and White must prevent Black from capturing on "f3" with 28 Nd5 Bxd5 29 Rxd5 Qxd5.

21...Qd7!

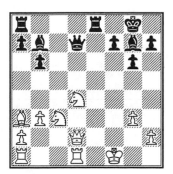

Diagram 192. Position after 21...Qd7

White resigned here. White has no adequate way of meeting Black's threat of 22...Qh3+. If 22 Ndb5 (the same continuation would occur against 22 Ncb5), then 22...Qh3+ 23 Kg1 Bh6 with the Bishop threatening White's Queen and going to "e3". If 22 Qf2, White loses his Queen after 22...Qh3+ 23 Kg1 Re1+! 24 Rxe1 Bxd4 (threatening 25...Qg2++) 25 Ne4 Bxf2+ 26 Kxf2 Qxh2+.

My Favorite Instructional Game

Stach (Germany) versus Snyder (USA)
ICCF Master Class Tournament, 1976–1977

Opening: Catalan

I use this game on a regular basis in my lessons for students. It contains many instructive elements such as rapid and effective piece development in the opening, gaining a strong outpost for a Knight, taking advantage of holes in the opponent's castled position, placing a Rook on the 7th rank and sacrificing to expose the enemy King to a mating attack.

1 d4 Nf6 2 c4 e6

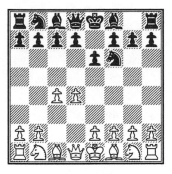

Diagram 193. Position after 2...e6

This move frees Black's Bishop on the "a3-f8" diagonal and supports the placement of a Pawn on "d5".

3 g3

White prepares to fianchetto his Bishop on "g2" and initiates the Catalan Opening. We will examine the Queen's Indian Defense with 3 Nf3 b6 and the Nimzo-Indian Defense with 3 Nc3 Bb4 in our next lessons.

3...d5

Black boldly occupies the center with a Pawn and attacks White's unprotected Pawn on "c4". Applying pressure to White's "c" Pawn is a very effective plan because, when using a fianchetto, White will be removing his Bishop from the "f1-a6" diagonal. Normally White's Bishop on the "f1-a6" diagonal would aid in the protection of his Pawn on "c4".

4 Bg2

White continues with his development by completing his fianchetto and ignoring Black's attack on the "c4" Pawn.

4...dxc4

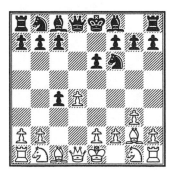

Diagram 194. Position after 4...dxc4

This doesn't win a Pawn. However, it will force White to use up valuable time to re-cover his Pawn. A reasonable alternative for Black was to continue with straightfor-ward development and play 4...Be7. The game may then have continued 5 Nf3 0-0 6 0-0 dxc4 7 Qc2 a6 8 Qxc4 (or 8 a4 Bd7 9 Qxc4 Bc6 10 Bg5 with an even game) b5 9 Qc2 Bb7 with an even game.

5 Qa4+

This fork will allow for the immediate recovery of White's Pawn. However, White must bring his Queen out early and consume valuable time. More common here is to forgo the immediate recovery of the Pawn and develop with 5 Nf3. A possible contin-uation may be 5...a6 6 0-0 Nc6 7 Nc3 (if 7 e3 then 7...Nd5 is strong) Rb8 8 e4 Be7 and Black stands well.

5...Nbd7

Black develops a piece to parry the check. From "d7" the Knight helps support Black to counter in the center by allowing a Pawn to go to "c5" or "e5". Another reasonable continuation was 5...Bd7 6 Qxc4 Bc6 7 Nf3 Bd5 8 Qd3 Be4 9 Qd1 c5 10 Nc3 Bc6 11 0-0 cxd4 12 Nxd4 Bxg2 13 Kxg2 with a balanced game.

6 Nd2

White's plan is to use the Knight on "d2" to capture the Pawn on "c4". This, along with White's Knight on "f3", would give White a strong foothold on the "e5" square.

More common alternatives here for White are either 6 Qxc4 a6 7 Nf3 b5 8 Qc2 Bb7 9 0-0 c5 with a good game for Black, or 6 Nf3 a6 7 Nc3 Rb8 8 Qxc4 b5 9 Qd3 Bb7 10 0-0 c5 with an even game.

6...c6

Black unpins his Knight on "d7" and threatens 7...b5, which would defend his Pawn on "c4" with an attack on White's Queen.

7 Qxc4

Diagram 195. Position after 7 Qxc4

White had little choice but to immediately recover his Pawn before Black could play 7…b5. Continuing with his plan of playing 7 Nxc4 would allow 7…b5 forking the Queen and Knight. See if you can find Black's best move here without looking at the next move in the game.

7…e5

This natural freeing move gives Black an excellent game. It immediately threatens to win a Pawn with 8…Nb6 (threatening White's Queen and attacking White's "d" Pawn a second time) and begins to open the "h3-c8" diagonal for Black's Bishop. Many players are tempted to attack White's Queen with 7…Nb6. However, this would place the Knight on an inferior square and does White's Queen no harm after 8 Qd3 c5 9 Ngf3.

8 dxe5

White meets Black's threat of 8…Nb6 by trading his "d" Pawn. However, playable was 8 Ngf3, which may have continued 8…exd4 9 Nxd4 (or if 9 Qxd4 then 9…Bc5) Ne5.

8…Nxe5

Black recovers his Pawn, centralizing his Knight with an attack on White's Queen.

9 Qc3

White gets his Queen out of attack while attacking Black's Knight.

9…Bd6

Diagram 196. Position after 9…Bd6

Black develops his Bishop while defending his Knight and preparing to castle.

10 Ngf3

White develops his Knight toward the center threatening Black's Knight on "e5" and preparing to castle. White would simply be weakening himself if he tried to gain a massive Pawn center with 10 f4 Ned7 11 e4 Qe7 12 e5 Bb4.

10...Qe7

Black brings his Queen to a flexible and active post where she defends the Knight on "e5".

11 0-0

White gets his King out of the center.

11...0-0

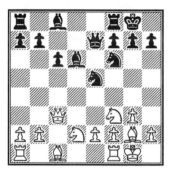

Diagram 197. Position after 11...0-0

Black also gets his King out of the center and will be able to bring his Rook onto an open central file. Here White must concern himself with Black playing 12...Nxf3+ 13 Bxf3 (defending the "e" Pawn against Black's Queen) Bh3 with a clear lead in development.

12 Nxe5

White prevents Black from playing 12...Nxf3+ as mentioned above.

12...Bxe5

Black recovers his Knight with an attack on White's Queen.

13 Qc2

White gets his Queen out of attack by placing the Queen where she is not easily attacked again.

13...Bg4

Diagram 198. Position after 13...Bg4

Black completes his minor piece development by aggressively developing his Bishop with an attack on White's "e" Pawn. Another reasonable move here was 13...Bc7 opening up the "e" file with an attack on White's "e" Pawn and anticipating an attack on Black's Bishop on "e5" by White's Knight. After 13...Bc7 the game Smyslov versus Keres, USSR Championship, 1950, continued, 14 e4 Re8 15 b3 Bg4 16 Nc4 Rad8 with a slightly more comfortable game for Black.

14 Nf3

White defends his "e" Pawn by blocking out Black's Bishop on "g4" and attacking Black's Bishop on "e5". It would have been slightly better to post the Knight more aggressively with 14 Nc4.

14...Bc7

Black preserves his Bishop pair by getting it out of attack by White's Knight. At the same time Black opens up the "e" file and prepares to apply pressure along it.

15 b3

White prepares to fianchetto his Bishop on the "a1-h8" diagonal. Developing the Bishop along its already opened diagonal did not work out so well in the game Junge versus Keres, Salzburg 1942, which continued 16 Be3 Rfe8 17 Rfe1 Ba5 18 Bd2 Bb6 19 Bc3 Rad8 with Black having a clear advantage.

15...Rfe8

Diagram 199. Position after 15...Rfe8

Black brings his Rook onto the open central file threatening White's "e" Pawn. This will provoke White to advance his "e" Pawn and weaken himself further on the White squares.

16 e3

White gets his "e" Pawn out of attack. If 16 Re1 then 16...Ba5 17 Bd2 Bb6 gives Black a nice advantage.

16...Rad8

Both of Black's Rooks are now being used on the two open center files. Note that every one of Black's pieces has been developed. We will see how Black takes advantage of his lead in development.

17 Nd4

White centralizes his Knight and opens up the diagonal for his Bishop on "g2". However, it would have been slightly better for White to complete his fianchetto with 17 Bb2, though Black still clearly comes out on top after 17...Qe4 18 Qxe4 Nxe4.

17...Be5

Diagram 200. Position after 17...Be5

Black centralizes his Bishop, pins White's Knight and is threatening 18...c5. Black has several small advantages, which add up to being a major advantage in the game for him. When I use this game in a lesson I ask my students to name them. See if you can see these advantages before moving on to the next paragraph.

Black's advantages in this position are: first, Black has a lead in development; second, Black has the Queenside Pawn majority; and third, White has white square weaknesses on the Kingside.

18 Bb2

White completes his fianchetto while removing the pin on his Knight.

18...c5

Black drives White's Knight away from its centralized post while forcing White to trade his most active minor piece. Also, by trading off the Bishop on "e5", Black opens up his Queen and Rook on the "e" file, which will support the placement of his Knight on the "e4" outpost.

19 Ne2

White gets his Knight out of attack by placing it where it can go to a more active square on either "c3" or "f4". If White plays 19 Nf3 then Black would have still continued with 19...Bxb2 20 Qxb2 Ne4 threatening 21...Bxf3 followed by 22...Nd2. If White plays 19 Nb5 then Black would do well to play 19...Bxb2 20 Qxb2 a6 21 Nc3 b5. And finally, if White tries pinning Black's "c" Pawn with 19 Ba3, then 19...Rc8! would prove most embarrassing to Black.

19...Bxb2

Black clears the way to support the placement of his Knight at its natural outpost on "e4".

20 Qxb2

White recovers his Bishop.

20...Ne4

Diagram 201. Position after 20...Ne4

Black takes the natural outpost for his Knight, which threatens 21...Rd2 with a fork on White's Queen and Knight.

21 Nf4

White removes his Knight from being a target to 21...Rd2 while posting it as actively as possible. See if you can find Black's best move here without looking at the next move in the game.

21...g5!

Diagram 202. Position after 21...g5

This move may seem like it weakens Black. However, with Black's initiative White will never have an opportunity to take advantage of any weakening of Black's Kingside Pawn structure. As a general rule you should keep this in mind: *"A weakness is only weak if it can be taken advantage of."* With this move Black will either drive the Knight away from its active post or force White into desperate measures to counterattack.

22 f3

Black counterattacks with a fork on White's Knight and Bishop. However, it would have been better for White to give up his good Bishop for White's Knight and submit to a clearly inferior position and play 22 Bxe4 Qxe4 23 Ng2.

Some interesting situations would have occurred if White retreated his Knight with 22 Nh3. I was planning on taking advantage of White's weakness on "f3" with 22...Nd2 (though 22...Rd2 23 Qc1 Red8 was also strong) 23 Rfc1 Nf3+ 24 Kh1 (White does not want to give up his important white squared Bishop with 24 Bxf3 Bxf3) Rd2 25 Rc2 (not 25 Qc3? because of 25...Bxh3 26 Bxh3 Rxf2 threatening an Arabian mate with 27...Rxh2++) Red8 26 Ng1 (or if 26 Rf1 then 26...Rxc2 27 Qxc2 Rd2 28 Qb1 Bxh3 29 Bxh3 Qxe3! and White cannot take the Queen with 30 fxe3 because once again Black has an Arabian mate with 30...Rxh2++) Rxc2 27 Qxc2 Rd2 28 Qc3 (if 28 Qc4 I had planned 28...Ne5 to meet 29 Qe4 with 29...Nd3! threatening a smothered mate on "f2") Rxf2 planning to meet 29 h3 with 29...Qd6! with the devastating threat of 30...Qxg3.

22...Rd2

Black posts his Rook actively on his 7th rank with an attack on White's Queen.

23 Qc1

White gets his Queen out of attack while tying down Black's Knight to the defense of his Rook on "d2".

23...gxf4

Diagram 203. Position after 23...gxf4

Black wins material by capturing White's Knight and attacking White's undefended "e" Pawn.

24 fxe4

White immediately recovers his minor piece. However, White would have lost quickly after 24 exf4 Qd6! 25 fxe4 Qd4+ 26 Kh1 Rxg2 27 Kxg2 Qxe4+ 28 Kg1 Qd4+ 29 Rf2 Re2 30 Qf1 Rxf2 31 Qxf2 Qxa1+. Also, if 24 gxf4 Bxf3 25 Rxf3 (if 25 Bxf3 then 25...Qh4 26 Bg2 Qg4) Qf6!, with the idea of playing 26...Kh8, followed by 27...Rg8.

24...fxe3

Black wins a Pawn while defending his Rook on "d2".

25 Qc3

Diagram 204. Position after 25 Qc3

White attacks Black's "e" Pawn and connects his Rooks. In light of what now happens it will be apparent that 25 Qe1 would have made the game last longer. See if you can find Black's best move here without looking at the next move in the game.

25...Rxg2+

This exchange sacrifice takes full advantage of White's white square weaknesses and exposes White's King to a deadly attack. Black resigned. In a correspondence game when you know your opponent's moves are rather forced you can send "if" moves to speed up the game. I sent if 26 Kxg2 Qxe4+ 27 Kg1 Bh3 28 Qb2 e2.

l e s s o n

19

A Massive Pawn Center

Walter Browne versus David Gliksman
Los Angeles, 1979

Opening: Queen's Indian Defense

Black makes the mistake of allowing White to obtain a massive Pawn center without an effective way to contest it. It is White's dominance in the center and spatial advantage that eventually forces the issue.

1 d4 Nf6 2 c4 e6 3 Nf3

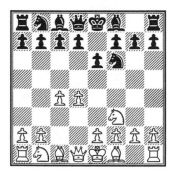

Diagram 205. Position after 3 Nf3

White develops a Knight toward the center. This avoids the pin, which occurs in the Nimzo-Indian Defense with 3 Nc3 Bb4.

3...b6

Black initiates the Queen's Indian Defense. He plans to fianchetto the Bishop along the "h1-a8" diagonal. In this opening it is important to control the "e4" square and not allow White to get a Pawn to "e4".

Other common moves here are 3...d5 4 Nc3 Be7, which transposes into the Queen's Gambit Declined, or 3...Bb4+ 4 Bd2 Qe7, which is known as the Bogo-Indian Defense.

4 a3

This move prevents Black's Bishop from going to "b4" and will support possible Queenside expansion with "b4". The most common move here is for White to counter Black's fianchetto by a fianchetto of his own with 4 g3. After 4 g3 the main line would continue 4...Bb7 5 Bg2 Be7 6 0-0 0-0 7 Nc3 Ne4 8 Qc2 Nxc3 9 Qxc3 c5 (or 9...f5 attacking the important "e4" square is also playable) 10 Rd1 d6 11 b3 Bf6 12 Bb2 Qe7 13 Qc2 Nc6 14 e4 e5 15 d5 Nd4 with about even chances.

4...Be7

Black develops his Bishop and prepares to castle. However, the passive development of the Bishop to "e7" at this stage was not the most accurate move. More exact was 4...Bb7 5 Nc3 d5 with an equal game.

5 Nc3

White develops his Knight toward the center where it may support the possible placement of a Pawn on "d5" or "e4".

5...Bb7?

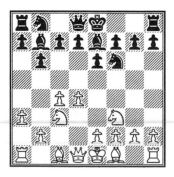

Diagram 206. Position after 5...Bb7

Black continues with his plan to fianchetto his Bishop without realizing the strength behind White's next move. It will become apparent soon that Black should have immediately taken a foothold in the center with 5...d5. See if you can find White's best move here without looking at the next move in the game.

6 d5!

This move cramps Black's game. Black's Bishop on "b7" is blocked and Black will be unable to prevent White from building his Pawn center further by getting a Pawn to "e4".

6...0-0

Black gets his King out of the center and brings his Rook to where it may be used on the "e" file later in the game. White still gets his nice Pawn center after 6...exd5 7 cxd5 0-0 8 e4 Re8 9 Bd3.

7 e4

White continues to build a massive Pawn center, increases his foothold on "d5" and frees his Bishop on "f1".

7...d6

Black opens up "d7" for possible use by a Knight and covers the "e5" square.

8 Bd3

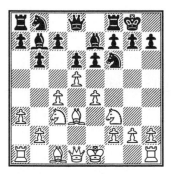

Diagram 207. Position after 8 Bd3

White develops his Bishop to its most aggressive available post and prepares to castle. However, 8 Be2 would have also given White a good game.

8...Nfd7

Black clears the "f6" square for use by his Bishop. The idea is for the Bishop on "f6" to get counterplay on the dark squares. If Black had played 8...Nbd7 then White could have strongly centralized his Knight with 9 Nd4! and Black cannot use his Bishop on "f6" to attack the Knight.

9 Be3

White completes his minor piece development, placing the Bishop on a flexible and active square.

9...Bf6

Black activates his Bishop along the "a1-h8" diagonal.

10 Rc1

Diagram 208. Position after 10 Rc1

White brings his Rook to a potentially more active file while defending his Knight on "c3". If White played 10 0-0 then Black would have been able to relieve some of the pressure by trading down and doubling White Pawns after 10...Bxc3 11 bxc3 Na6 with Black having a foothold on "c5" for a Knight.

10...a5

Black anticipates White's plan to expand on the Queenside with "b4". Therefore, he plans to obtain an open file for his Rook on the "a" file if this happens.

11 b4?

This immediate expansion on the Queenside is premature and falls right into Black's plan of obtaining an open "a" file for his Rook. White should have played 11 0-0 which might have continued 11...Na6 12 Nd4 with White clearly being dominant in the center.

11...axb4

Black opens up the "a" file for his Rook.

12 axb4

White recovers his Pawn.

12...Ne5

Diagram 209. Position after 12...Ne5

Black seeks to relieve some of the pressure by trading Knights. Though this in general is a good idea, the drawback is that Black will end up with a Bishop that is exposed to attack on "e5".

13 Nxe5

White removes Black's aggressively posted Knight while bringing Black's Bishop to a square where it is a target.

13...Bxe5

Black recovers his piece.

14 0-0

White gets his King out of the center before driving away Black's Bishop on "e5". Weaker would have been 14 f4 because of 14...Bxc3+ 15 Rxc3 Qh4+ 16 g3 Qf6.

14...Nd7

Black develops his Knight and completes his minor piece development.

15 f4

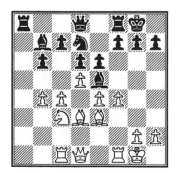

Diagram 210. Position after 15 f4

White drives Black's Bishop off its centralized post while gaining more space in the center and Kingside. White has built up a massive Pawn center and will utilize his spatial advantage.

15...Bf6

Black gets his Bishop out of attack. It would have been slightly better for Black to try to relieve some of the pressure by trading down with 15...Bxc3 16 Rxc3 Qe7. However, Black probably didn't like the prospects of giving up the Bishop pair and still being cramped. See if you can find White's best move here without looking at the next move in the game.

16 Nb5!

This is a wonderful post for the Knight and a move for all seasons! It ties Black's Queen to the defense of the "c" Pawn, relieves White's Rook on "c1" of the defense of the Knight, opens up further the influence of White's Rook on the "c" file and allows for a possible posting of a piece on "d4".

16...Re8

Black brings his Rook onto the "e" file.

17 Qc2

This is another move which does many things. It backs up the Bishop along the "b1-h7" diagonal, sets up a possible discovered attack on Black's "h" Pawn, connects the Rooks along the 1st rank, covers the 2nd rank (which prevents the likelihood of Black's Rook penetrating to White's 2nd rank) and adds support for the possible advance of White's "c" Pawn.

17...Ba6?

Diagram 211. Position after 17...Ba6

Since the "h1-a8" diagonal is blocked for this Bishop it is very understandable that it wants to seek greener pastures. The idea of exchanging Black's inactive Bishop for

White's awesome Knight on "b5" is logical. However, White's threat of opening up the "b1-h7" diagonal with an attack on Black's "h" Pawn should have been dealt with. Therefore, 17...g6 was better.

18 dxe6?

White's idea is to bring Black's Rook to a square where it will be a target. However, the Rook is actually more active on "e6". It would be stronger to immediately attack Black's Bishop on "f6" and open up the "b1-h7" diagonal with 18 e5! After 18 e5! the game might have continued 18...dxe5 (if 18...Bxb5 then 19 exf6 is very strong because it threatens the Bishop on "b5" and 20 Bxh7+, or if 18...exd5 then White opens the "c" file with 19 cxd5 and would be winning after 19...Bxb5 20 Bxb5 dxe5 21 Qxc7) 19 Bxh7+ Kh8 20 dxe6 exf4 (if 20...Rxe6 then 21 Be4 is strong, transposing into the actual game) 21 Bxf4 Bxb5 22 exf7 Rf8 23 Bg8 and White is clearly winning.

18...Rxe6

Black recovers his Pawn. It would have been weaker to play 18...fxe6 because of 19 e5 dxe5 20 Bxh7+ Kh8 21 Be4.

19 e5

White forces the opening of lines and attacks the Bishop on "f6" and Black's Pawn on "h7".

19...dxe5?

This move eliminates the threat against Black's Bishop on "f6". Though Black would still have serious problems, he misses his opportunity to minimize White's advantage with 19...Bxb5, which might have continued 20 Bxh7+ (also playable for White would be 20 cxb5 when Black does best to defend with 20...g6) Kh8 21 cxb5 g6 (if 21...dxe5 then 22 Bf5 Rd6 23 Qxc7 Qxc7 24 Rxc7) 22 Rf3! Kxh7 23 exf6 Ra3 24 Qf2.

20 Bxh7+

White recovers his Pawn and begins to expose Black's King to attack.

20...Kf8

Diagram 212. Position after 20...Kf8

Black gets his King out of check while trying to keep as much of a shield around his King as possible. See if you can find White's best move here without looking at the next move in the game.

21 Be4!

White centralizes his Bishop on a very active square and attacks Black's Rook on "a8".

21...c6

Black blocks White's attack on his Rook while attacking Black's Knight. This may lose a Pawn, but Black didn't have anything better. For example, if Black moved his Rook out of attack with 21...Rb8 then Black is crushed after 22 Bd5 Re8 23 Na7 Bb7 24 Bxb7 Rxb7 25 Nc6 Qa8 26 Qh7. See if you can find White's best move here without looking at the next move in the game.

22 f5

This move drives Black's Rook away from the defense of the "c" Pawn, which results in the win of a Pawn and quick collapse of Black's game.

22...Re7

Black gets his Rook away from attack by White's Pawn.

23 Bxc6

White wins a Pawn and attacks the Black Rook on "a8".

23...Rc8

Diagram 213. Position after 23...Rc8

Black gets his Rook out of attack by placing it on the half-open "c" file and attacking White's undefended Bishop on "c6". See if you can find White's best move here without looking at the next move in the game.

24 Qe4!

White centralizes his Queen to defend and maintain his Bishop's active post on "c6".

24...Bxb5

Black attempts to relieve some of the pressure by making an even exchange. However, this will do him little good since he is down a Pawn and White's position is overwhelming. If Black tries attacking White's Bishop on "c6" with 24...Nb8, then 25 Rfd1 attacking Black's Queen would have been embarrassing.

25 Bxb5

White recovers his minor piece.

25...Qc7

Diagram 214. Position after 25...Qc7

Black moves the Queen off the open "d" file and brings her to where he hopes she will do some good by being more actively located. See if you can find White's best move here without looking at the next move in the game.

26 g4!

Black resigned here. He is defenseless against White's threat of 27 g5. If Black plays 26...g5 White will crack open Black's Kingside with 27 fxg6 e.p. Or if, 26...Ree8 then 27 g5 Be7 28 Qh4 Kg8 29 Rf3 with the idea of 30 Rh3 followed by 31 Qh8++.

l e s s o n

20

Weak Pawns

Arthur Spiller versus Robert Snyder
California, 1974

Opening: Nimzo-Indian Defense

Preparing well in advance for the endgame is often an important part of planning that is overlooked. In this game Black gives White three isolated Pawns and then applies pressure to them.

1 d4 Nf6 2 c4 e6 3 Nc3

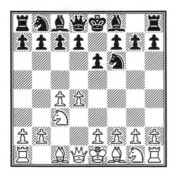

Diagram 215. Position after 3 Nc3

White develops a Knight and threatens to obtain a dominating Pawn center with 4 e4.

3...Bb4

This is known as the Nimzo-Indian Defense. Black aggressively develops his Bishop and pins White's Knight on "c3". This prevents White from playing 4 e4.

4 a3

This is known as the Sämisch Variation. White forces Black to either make an unfavorable retreat or exchange his Bishop for White's Knight.

4...Bxc3+

Black gets his Bishop out of attack. He gives up the Bishop pair but doubles White's Pawns. Black's Bishop would be trapped after 4...Ba5?? 5 b4 Bb6 6 c5.

5 bxc3

Diagram 216. Position after 5 bxc3

White recovers his piece.

5...c5

Black begins to counter White's Pawn center by striking at the center with a Pawn. This move frees Black's Queen along the "a5-d8" diagonal. In many cases this diagonal can be used effectively.

6 f3

This is White's most aggressive variation. White prepares to increase his Pawn center further with 7 e4. Also playable for White here is 6 e3, which might continue 6...b6 (Black plans to increase his foothold on "e4" through the use of a fianchetto) 7 Bd3 Bb7 8 Nf3 Ne4 9 Qc2 f5 10 0-0 0-0 11 Nd2 Qh4 12 f3 (weak would be 12 g3 because Black could play 12...Nxd2! planning to meet 13 gxh4? with 13...Nf3+ 14 Kg2 Nxd4+ 15 Kg3 Nxc2) Nxd2 13 Bxd2 Nc6 with an even game. Weak would be 6 dxc5? because of 6...Qa5 and if 7 Qd4? then 7...Nc6 8 Qe3 Ne4!

6...d5

This move continues to build a Pawn center, attacks White's unprotected Pawn on "c4", helps to free Black's Queenside pieces and prevents White from playing 7 e4.

7 cxd5

White gets rid of his doubled Pawns and the attack on his unprotected "c" Pawn through this exchange. Passive would have been 7 e3, which might have continued 7...0-0 8 Bd3 Qc7 with an excellent game for Black.

7...Nxd5

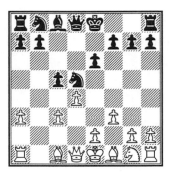

Diagram 217. Position after 7...Nxd5

This is Black's most aggressive move. Black recovers his Pawn, actively posts his Knight in the center and threatens 8...Nxc3. However, 7...exd5 is also playable with an even game.

8 dxc5

White will force Black to take the time to recover his Pawn, which was his best way of meeting Black's threat on "c3". If White defended his Pawn on "c3" with 8 Qd3 the game might have continued 8...cxd4 9 cxd4 Nc6 10 e4 Nb6 11 Be3 0-0 12 Ne2 Ne5 13 Qb3 Nec4 with about equal chances.

8...f5

Black attacks the important "e4" square in anticipation of White placing a Pawn there. If 8...Qa5, White is clearly better after 9 e4 Ne7 (not 9...Nxc3? because of 10 Qd2 and if 10...Qxc5? then 11 Bb2 Na4 12 Rc1) 10 Ne2.

9 c4

White plans to drive Black's Knight away from the center. However, this favorably opens up the "a1-h8" diagonal for Black. Either developing with 9 Nh3 0-0, or striking at the center with 9 e4 fxe4 10 Qc2 e3 11 Bd3 Nd7 would have been better. See if you can find Black's best move here without looking at the next move in the game.

9...Qf6!

Black actively brings his Queen into play along the "a1-h8" diagonal, threatening White's Rook on "a1".

Diagram 218. Position after 9...Qf6

10 Bd2

White develops his Bishop, covers "c3" and defends his Rook on "a1" with his Queen. Also to be considered was 10 Bg5 Qxg5 11 cxd5 f4.

10...Nc3

Black plays aggressively getting his Knight out of attack while threatening White's Queen.

11 Qc1

White gets his Queen out of attack while keeping the Rook on "a1" protected and threatening Black's Knight on "c3". White would have lost material after 11 Qc2? Ne4! (with a discovered attack on White's unprotected Rook on "a1") 12 Rd1 Qh4+ 13 g3 Nxg3. Also, White didn't like the option of giving up his Bishop pair and ability to castle after 11 Bxc3 Qxc3+ 12 Kf2 f4 13 g3 e5.

11...Na4

Black gets his Knight out of attack while attacking Black's weak Pawn on "c5" and keeping White's Queen tied down to the Rook on "a1".

12 f4?

White opens the "f3" square for the development of his Knight and tries to get a foothold on the important "e5" square. However, it would have been better to play 12 Rb1, freeing his Queen from the defense of the Rook and placing the Rook on the half-open "b" file with pressure on Black's "b" Pawn. After 12 Rb1 Black would still have had a good game after 12...Nc6 with the idea of placing his Pawn on "e5".

12...Nc6

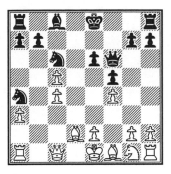

Diagram 219. Position after 12...Nc6

Black develops his Knight toward the center and prepares support for an attack in the center with 13...e5.

13 Nf3

White continues with his plan of developing his Knight toward the center in the fight for the important "e5" square.

13...e5

Black attacks in the center and further opens the diagonal for his Bishop on "c8". However, 13...Nxc5, immediately recovering his Pawn and threatening 14...Nb3 and gaining control over "e4", was stronger.

14 fxe5

White eliminates Black's menacing "e" Pawn, which threatened to go to "e4".

14...Nxe5

Black recovers his Pawn, bringing his Knight into the center.

15 Nxe5?

This exchange only brings Black's Queen to a stronger square where she nicely covers the center. It would have been better to play 15 Bg5 attacking Black's Queen.

15...Qxe5

Black recovers his Knight and brings his Queen to an active location in the center.

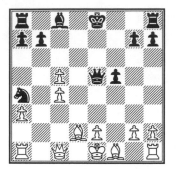

Diagram 220. Position after 15...Qxe5

16 Bf4

White places his Bishop on the more active "h2-b8" diagonal while attacking Black's Queen.

16...Qxc5

Black recovers his Pawn while getting his Queen out of attack. White has three isolated Pawns and it will be a while before White is able to get his King castled. White's Bishop pair is not enough compensation.

17 Qe3+

White wants to trade off his less active Queen for Black's more active Queen. However, this will simply leave White in an inferior endgame with weak Pawns. If White avoided exchanging Queens with 17 Rb1, White would have great difficulty castling after 17...0-0 18 e3 Qc6 19 Qd2 b6.

17...Qxe3

Black doesn't mind trading Queens, which will also place White's Bishop on an inferior square, blocking his "e" Pawn.

18 Bxe3

White recovers his Queen.

18...Be6

Black begins to take advantage of White's weak isolated Pawns by developing his Bishop and attacking White's Pawn on "c4".

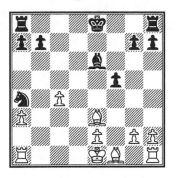

Diagram 221. Position after 18...Be6

19 Bd4

Often the best defense is a good offense. White counters Black's attack on his "c" Pawn by bringing his Bishop to a central square where it attacks Black's unprotected Pawn on "g7" and unblocks the "e" Pawn.

19...0-0

Black defends his Pawn on "g7" while getting his King out of the center and activating his Kingside Rook.

20 e3

White frees his Bishop on "f1" which defends his Pawn on "c4". The Pawn on "e3" also defends his actively posted Bishop on "d4". See if you can find Black's best move here without looking at the next move in the game.

20...Rac8

Black brings his Rook into play and increases the pressure on White's isolated "c" Pawn.

21 Rc1

White defends his "c" Pawn, which is attacked by two pieces. If White went Pawn grabbing with 21 Bxa7 his Bishop's retreat would have been cut off with 21...b6. See if you can find Black's best move here without looking at the next move in the game.

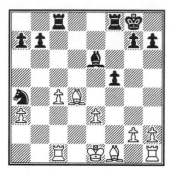

Diagram 222. Position after 21 Rc1

21...Nc5!

Black blockades White's weak "c" Pawn, blocks White's attack on the Pawn on "a7" and brings his Knight to an excellent post where it attacks White's weak squares on "b3", "d3" and "e4".

22 Be2

White finally is able to get his Bishop developed and prepares to castle.

22...Rfd8

Black brings his Kingside Rook into play on the open "d" file. Black plans to improve the position of this Rook through an interesting maneuver to take advantage of White's weak isolated Pawns.

Black could have immediately broken the ice and won a Pawn with 22...Nb3 23 Rb1 (if 23 Rc2 then 23...Nxd4 24 exd4 Rfd8 would win a Pawn) Nxd4 24 exd4 Bxc4. However, Black's plan in the game was to further increase pressure before forcing the issue.

23 Rc2

In anticipation of White's Knight going to "b3", White removes his Rook from "c1" where it would be attacked.

23...Rd6

Black brings his Rook to his 3rd rank where it can shift into play to attack White's weaknesses on the Queenside. This move also gives Black the option of doubling his

Rooks. A simple and good alternative for Black was to unpin and defend the Knight on "c5" a second time by playing 23…b6.

24 0-0

Diagram 223. Position after 24 0-0

White removes his King from the center and activates his Kingside Rook.

24…Ra6

Black threatens White's isolated Pawn on "a3", provoking White to retreat his Bishop to a less active square to defend it. Again, a good alternative for Black was to play 24…b6 as previously mentioned.

25 Bb2

White defends his isolated "a" Pawn which was threatened. However, it would have been better to play more aggressively with 25 Bf3, which might have continued 25…Ne4 26 Bxe4 fxe4 27 Rb1 Rc7. This would have minimized Black's advantage by increasing the chances for a draw by having Bishops of opposite colors.

25…Rb6

Now that White's Bishop has retreated to "b2" Black repositions his Rook to penetrate on the open "b" file. This now has the added advantage that White's Rook will be tied down to the defense of the Bishop on "b2".

26 Rd1?

This does not improve the location of White's Rook. White should have played 26 Bd4 in anticipation of Black's upcoming Rook penetration. The Bishop would have defended the isolated "e" Pawn and been more active on "d4". After 26 Bd4 White would plan to meet 26…Rb3 with 27 Ra1 defending the "a" Pawn. See if you can find Black's best move here without looking at the next move in the game.

26...Rb3

This was the whole idea of Black's plan. On "b3" the Rook attacks both the isolated "a" and "e" Pawns, while tying down White's Rook to the defense of the Bishop on "b2".

27 Kf2?

Diagram 224. Position after 27 Kf2

In an attempt to defend his "e" Pawn and use his King as an active fighting piece White has made his King a target on "f2". It would have been better to play 27 Bc1 to defend the "e" Pawn and to relieve White's Rook from the task of defending the Bishop. See if you can find Black's best move here without looking at the next move in the game.

27...b5!

Black attacks White's weak "c" Pawn again, which is now beyond salvation. Of course White cannot play 28 cxb5?? because of the discovered attack with 28...Ne4+ (taking advantage of White's King being on "f2") 29 Ke1 Rxc2.

28 Rd4

White attempts to defend his "c" Pawn. However, it does no good.

28...bxc4

Black wins the "c" Pawn.

29 Rdxc4?

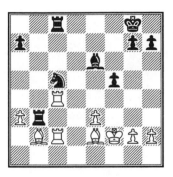

Diagram 225. Position after 29 Rdxc4

This is tactically unsound and loses at least a piece. White would have lasted longer with 29 Bc1. Here White hopes for 29...Bxc4?? 30 Bxc4+ Kf8 31 Bxb3. See if you can find Black's best move here without looking at the next move in the game.

29...Ne4+

This clearly demonstrates why 27 Kf2 was weak. The discovered attack on the "c" file wins material.

30 Ke1

White gets his King out of check.

30...Rxc4

Black wins material by taking advantage of White's Rook on "c2" being an over-worked defender (defending pieces both on "b2" and "c4").

31 Bxc4

White recovers the Rook.

31...Bxc4

Diagram 226. Position after 31...Bxc4

White resigned here. After 32 Rxc4 Rxb2 White has lost a piece.

Deep Positional Sacrifice

Richter (Germany) versus Snyder (USA)
ICCF Master Class Tournament, 1976–1979

Opening: Nimzo-Indian

The first 20 moves of this game is well-known book analysis. It is common for Masters to follow opening analysis from books for the first 20 or 30 moves. Black sacrifices a piece for long-term positional pressure, thereby testing an important opening line.

1 d4 Nf6 2 c4 e6 3 Nc3 Bb4 4 Qc2

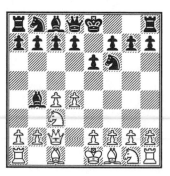

Diagram 227. Position after 4 Qc2

This is known as the Classical or Capablanca Variation. White defends his Knight on "c3" with his Queen, with the idea of avoiding doubled Pawns by being able to recapture with his Queen if Black plays Bxc3. Also, from "c2" the Queen may add support to further expansion in the center with "e4". One drawback is that White uses a move to bring his Queen out early. Another drawback is that by removing the Queen from "d1", White has lessened control of the important "d" file and support of his Pawn on "d4".

4...d5

Black places a Pawn in the center with an attack on White's unprotected "c" Pawn. This move also helps free Black's Queenside pieces. Other reasonable moves here are 4...0-0 or 4...c5.

5 a3

White attacks Black's Bishop to either force it to retreat to a less active square or be exchanged for the Knight on "c3", which would give White the Bishop pair. However, the most common move here is 5 cxd5, which might continue 5...exd5 6 Bg5 h6 7 Bh4 0-0 with about even chances.

5...Bxc3+

Black takes care of the attack on his Bishop by exchanging it for White's Knight on "c3". It would have been inconsistent to lose time by retreating with 5...Be7 6 Nf3 0-0 7 Bg5 with a slight edge for White.

6 Qxc3

White recovers his piece without doubling his Pawns.

6...Ne4

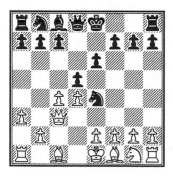

Diagram 228. Position after 6...Ne4

Black attacks White's Queen while actively posting his Knight in the center.

7 Qc2

White gets his Queen out of attack while keeping her on an active and flexible post with pressure on White's Knight on "e4".

7...c5

Black aggressively attacks in the center, threatening White's Pawn on "d4" and freeing the Queen along the "a5-d8" diagonal.

8 dxc5

White gets rid of the threat on his "d" Pawn. This move also will force Black to take time to recover his own Pawn. Attempting to drive away White's Knight with 8 f3?? doesn't work because of 8...Qh4+ 9 g3 Nxg3.

8...Nc6

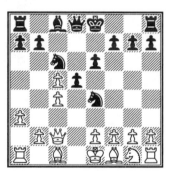

Diagram 229. Position after 8...Nc6

Black continues with his minor piece development. It would be a serious error for Black to have immediately recovered his Pawn with 8...Nxc5?, because after 9 cxd5 Qxd5? 10 b4 Black is losing a piece.

9 cxd5

This exchange allows White's Queen to defend his Pawn on "c5". This will force Black to prove that his superior minor piece development is worth his sacrificed Pawn.

9...exd5

Black recovers his Pawn and opens up the "h3-c8" diagonal for his Bishop.

10 Nf3

White develops his Knight toward the center in preparation to play "b4". It would have been a blunder to immediately play 10 b4?? because of 10...Qf6!, attacking White's Rook on "a1" and Pawn on "f2".

10...Bf5

Black develops his Bishop to the active "b1-h7" diagonal. This sets up the possibility of a discovered attack on White's Queen, which is on the same diagonal.

11 b4

White reinforces the protection of his "c" Pawn and prepares to fianchetto his Bishop to "b2".

11...0-0

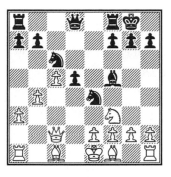

Diagram 230. Position after 12...0-0

Black gets his King out of the center. Tempting but weak would have been the discovered attack with 11...Ng3. White comes out on top after 12 Qb2 Nxh1 13 Qxg7 Rf8 14 Bh6 Qe7 15 Qxf8+ Qxf8 16 Bxf8 Kxf8 17 g3 and Black's Knight is trapped on "h1".

12 Bb2

Black completes his fianchetto, placing the Bishop on the long "a1-h8" diagonal.

12...b6

Black begins to attack White's Pawn chain with the idea of breaking it up. Once again it would not be good to play 12...Ng3 because of 13 Qc3 d4 14 Nxd4 Nxd4 15 fxg3.

13 b5

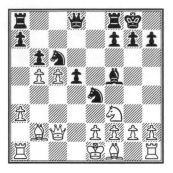

Diagram 231. Position after 13 b5

White plays aggressively, attacking Black's Knight on "c6" with the hopes of moving his Pawn to "c6" and creating an even stronger Pawn chain. A reasonable alternative for White would have been 13 Qa4 Qc7.

13...bxc5

Black does best to sacrifice his Knight. If 13...Na5, White will obtain a very strong Pawn chain after 14 c6.

14 bxc6

White has little choice but to accept the Knight sacrifice.

14...Qa5+

Black brings his Queen into play and connects his Rooks. This will force White's Knight to retreat to a less active square where it will be pinned.

15 Nd2

This was White's only move to avoid massive material loss.

15...Rab8

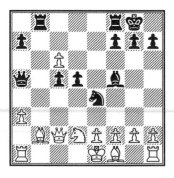

Diagram 232. Position after 15...Rab8

Black places his Rook on an open file attacking White's Bishop on "b2". As a result, Black threatens to regain his sacrificed piece with 16...Nxd2 17 Qxd2 Qxd2+ 18 Kxd2 Rxb2+.

16 Rd1

White brings his Rook into play defending his Knight on "d2". In the event of exchanges on "d2" White will be able to recapture with his Rook to defend his Bishop on "b2".

16...d4

Black blocks White's Bishop on the "a1-h8" diagonal and cramps White in the center to hinder his Kingside development.

17 c7

White returns a Pawn to distract Black's Queen from her strong pin on the "e1-a4" diagonal. It is worth returning the Pawn to relieve some of the pressure.

17...Qxc7

Black eliminates White's menacing Pawn.

18 Nxe4

White attempts to relieve pressure by making an even exchange.

18...Bxe4

Diagram 233. Position after 18...Bxe4

Black recovers his piece and attacks White's Queen.

19 Qd2

White gets his Queen out of attack while keeping the Bishop on "b2" protected. White would lose quickly after 19 Qxe4?? Qa5+ 20 Rd2 (if 20 Bc3 then 20...dxc3 21 Qc2 Rb2 wins easily) Rxb2 21 Qd3 c4 and White must lose his Queen or get checkmated.

19...Rfe8

Black brings his Rook effectively into play on the half-open "e" file. Up to here both sides have been following known opening theory. Materially, White is ahead, having a Bishop for a Pawn. In return Black has enormous pressure. All of Black's pieces are effectively in play, while White is undeveloped on the Kingside and his King is in the center. In theory White should be able to hold, but in practice his position is very difficult to handle.

20 f3

White drives Black's Bishop away from its strong post on "e4". However, this weakens the "e3" square. In the game Grigorian versus Gulko, USSR 1975, White played 20 h4 to try to free up his Kingside by getting his Rook into play. The game continued 20...Rb6 (immediately playing 20...Qb7 attacking the Bishop on "b2" and Pawn on "g2" was more direct) 21 Rh3 (stronger was 21 Bc1 removing the Bishop from being a target on the "b" file) Qb7 attacking the Bishop on "b2" and Pawn on "g2".

20...Bc6

Black gets his Bishop out of attack. However, it would have been stronger to maintain the Bishop on a center square with 20...Bd5.

21 Rc1

White repositions his Rook, attacking Black's backward "c" Pawn. White will try to restrain and attack Black's aggressively posted Pawns.

21...Qb6

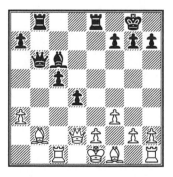

Diagram 234. Position after 21...Qb6

Black defends his "c" Pawn while threatening White's Bishop on "b2".

22 Ba1

White gets his Bishop out of attack.

22...Bd5

Black repositions his Bishop in the center where it may support the advance of the "c" Pawn. It becomes apparent now why playing Bd5 back on move 20 was stronger.

23 Qc2

In an attempt to put pressure on Black's Pawns, White threatens Black's "c" Pawn. However, this allows Black to advance his Pawns, making them stronger and more dangerous to White. White should have been willing to give up a Pawn to free his Kingside with 23 e4 f5 24 Be2.

23...c4

Black gets his Pawn out of attack while aggressively advancing it with the idea of further cramping White's position.

24 e4

Diagram 235. Position after 24 e4

It was necessary for White to try to get some space in the center and free his Bishop on "f1". Black now has two connected passed Pawns and continues to have considerable pressure for his sacrificed Bishop.

24...d3

Black attacks White's Queen and prevents White's Bishop from being developed along the "f1-a6" diagonal.

25 Qc3

White gets his Queen out of attack and threatens 26 Qxg7++.

25...f6

Black blocks White's Queen and Bishop along the "a1-h8" diagonal and stops White's mate threat.

26 Qd4

With White's King trapped in the center, White seeks a Queen trade to reduce the danger.

26...Qxd4

Black begins a combination which wins a Pawn and gives him good piece play.

27 Bxd4

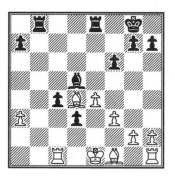

Diagram 236. Position after 27 Bxd4

White recovers his Queen. See if you can find Black's best move here without looking at the next move in the game.

27...Bxe4

Black continues with his combination, which wins a Pawn.

28 Kd2

White removes his King from the "e" file where he is exposed to a possible discovered attack. White also uses his King to help blockade Black's passed Pawns. White is now threatening to win Black's Bishop with 29 fxe4 and a Pawn with 29 Rxc4. If White played 28 fxe4 then Black would have recovered his piece with a great position after 28...Rxe4+ followed by 29...Rxd4.

28...Bd5

Black gets his Bishop out of attack and defends his "c" Pawn.

29 h4

White expands on the Kingside in an attempt to free his Rook, and eventually his Bishop on "f1".

29...h5

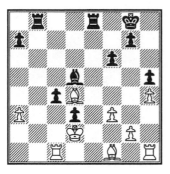

Diagram 237. Position after 29...h5

Black restricts the further advance of White's "h" Pawn and hinders White from playing "g4".

30 Rh3

White's idea is to bring the Rook into play on the 3rd rank to defend the "f" Pawn so that White can advance his "g" Pawn. However, it doesn't turn out to be tactically sound.

30...Kf7

Black brings his King to a more active square in line with the concept of using your King as an active fighting piece in the endgame. This is an extremely difficult position to handle for White, so Black didn't mind making a conservative move that helped improve the position of his King.

31 g4?

White is trying to expand on the Kingside and free his Bishop on "f1". However, this move loses a Pawn. It would have been better to reposition his Bishop to defend on the Queenside and play 31 Bc3. The idea would be to play 32 Bb4, blocking the ability of Black's Rook to penetrate on the "b" file.

31...hxg4

This is the beginning of a combination that wins a Pawn.

32 fxg4

Diagram 238. Position after 32 fxg4

White recovers his Pawn. See if you can find Black's best move here without looking at the next move in the game.

32...Re4

Black forks White's Bishop and Pawn.

33 Bc3

White gets his Bishop out of attack while maintaining control over "b2". If White played 33 Bxa7 it would allow Black's Rook to penetrate with 33...Rb2+, which might continue 34 Kc3 Rb3+ 35 Kd2 Rxg4 36 Bc5 Bg2.

33...Rxg4

Black wins a Pawn. Black now has three Pawns for the Bishop and a great position!

34 Re1

White tries to place his Rook on a more active file. However, the Rook will end up having little to do on the "e" file. It would have been better to get the "h" Pawn out of attack and use it aggressively with 34 h5. After 34 h5 Black would still do best to penetrate with his Rook and play 34...Rb3 attacking the "a" Pawn.

34...Rb3

Diagram 239. Position after 34...Rb3

Black penetrates with his Rook threatening White's "a" Pawn.

35 a4

White gets his Pawn out of attack.

35...Ra3

This places the Rook behind White's "a" Pawn threatening it again, while allowing for the possibility of the Rook attacking on Black's 7th rank.

36 a5

White places his "a" Pawn on a square where it is protected. Interesting would have been 36 Re7+ Kxe7 37 Bb4+ Kf7 38 Bxa3. However, after 38...Rf4! Black is winning a piece. See if you can find Black's best move here without looking at the next move in the game.

36...Bg2!

Diagram 240. Position after 36...Bg2

This attack on White's Rook and Bishop forces the win of material. Second best, but also good enough to win, would have been 36...Ra2+ 37 Kd1 Bc6 with the idea of 38...Bd4+.

37 h5

This is desperation. No matter what White did he couldn't have avoided the loss of material.

37...Bxf1

Black clears "g2" for his Rook to penetrate to his 7th rank.

38 Rxf1

White recovers his Bishop.

38...Rg2+

Diagram 241. Position after 38...Rg2+

Black posts his Rook actively on his 7th rank, attacking White's King and driving it away from the protection of his Bishop on "c3".

39 Ke3

White gets his King out of check, placing it on its most active available square.

39...Rxc3

Black wins a Bishop, leaving White down three Pawns with a hopeless position. White resigned here.

Queenside Pawn Majority

Richard Fowell versus Robert Snyder
Los Angeles, 1974

Opening: **Nimzo-Indian**

Black uses his Queenside Pawn majority to win in a Bishops of opposite color endgame.

1 d4 Nf6 2 c4 e6 3 Nc3 Bb4 4 e3

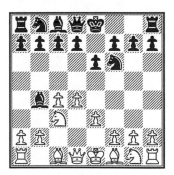

Diagram 242. Position after 4 e3

This is known as the Rubenstein Variation and is White's most popular fourth move. White defends his "e" Pawn a second time while opening the "f1-a6" diagonal for the Bishop on "f1".

4...0-0

Black removes his King from the center before striking at the center with his Pawns.

5 Bd3

White develops his Bishop to the long "b1-h7" diagonal.

5...d5

Black places a Pawn in the center, which also assists in freeing his Queenside pieces.

6 Nf3

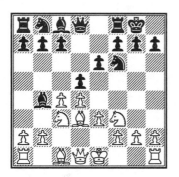

Diagram 243. Position after 6 Nf3

White develops a Knight toward the center and clears the way for his King to castle.

6...c5

Black uses a second Pawn to attack in the center. It would be weak to place a Knight in front of the "c" Pawn with 6...Nc6, which would cramp Black's game.

7 0-0

White gets his King out of the center.

7...Nc6

Black develops his second Knight toward the center. Both sides have three out of four of their minor pieces developed, castled Kings and good Pawn centers. Both sides must solve the problem of how to develop their Queenside Bishops.

8 a3

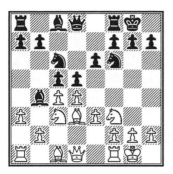

Diagram 244. Position after 8 a3

This will force Black's Bishop to either exchange on "c3" or retreat.

8...Bxc3

Black decides to give up the Bishop pair and double White's Pawns. This is the most common book move played here. However, another interesting move is to retreat the Bishop with 8...Ba5, which might continue 9 cxd5 exd5 10 dxc5 Bxc3 11 bxc3 Bg4 12 c4 Ne5 with about even chances.

9 bxc3

White recovers his piece. White's doubled Pawns are temporary since his "c" Pawn is soon to be exchanged for Black's "d" Pawn. This move also has the advantage of capturing toward the center, which makes White's Pawn center stronger. It also will give White's Bishop on "c1" more possibilities for development.

9...dxc4

This removes White's Bishop from the effective "b1-h7" diagonal and relieves the "e" Pawn and Queen from the task of defending the "d" Pawn. This is part of Black's plan to prepare for the advance of his "e" Pawn.

10 Bxc4

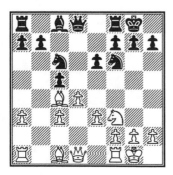

Diagram 245. Position after 10 Bxc4

White recovers his Pawn. See if you can find Black's best move here without look-ing at the next move in the game.

10...Qc7

The Queen has an excellent post on "c7". From "c7" she supports Black's plan to attack in the center with "e5", is placed on the long "h2-b8" and "a5-d8" diagonals, covers Black's 2nd rank and has the possibility of being used in a discovered attack on the "c" file.

The natural looking 10...Qe7 would prove inferior after 11 a4 b6 12 Ba3.

11 Qe2

White brings his Queen into play, defending his Bishop on "c4", supporting the possible advance of his "e" Pawn and connecting his Rooks on the 1st rank. However, the Queen can easily become a target here, which will be pointed out later in the game.

It would be weak to obtain isolated and doubled Pawns by going Pawn grabbing with 11 dxc5. Black then would have a choice of playing 11...Ne4, which would re-cover his Pawn with a nice position, or playing 11...Rd8 bringing the Rook onto the open "d" file and attacking White's Queen. White still would have no hope of keeping his extra Pawn.

The most popular move here is 11 Bd3. This places the Bishop on the effective "b1-h7" diagonal while removing it from being a possible target on the "c" file. After 11 Bd3 the game might continue 11...e5 12 Qc2 Re8 with an even game.

See if you can find Black's best move here without looking at the next move in the game.

11...e5

Black frees his Bishop on "c8" along the "h3-c8" diagonal and uses his Pawn to aggressively attack in the center.

12 d5

Diagram 246. Position after 12 d5

White removes the pressure from his "d" Pawn while using it aggressively by attacking Black's Knight on "c6". Exchanging on "e5" with 12 dxe5 Nxe5 13 Nxe5 Qxe5 would leave White with two isolated Pawns and Black having the Queenside Pawn majority and more active pieces. White's Bishop pair would not be enough to compensate for this.

See if you can find Black's best move here without looking at the next move in the game.

12...e4

Black counters White's threat on his Knight by attacking White's Knight on "f3". If Black got his Knight out of attack with either 12...Na5 or 12...Ne7, White would get a strong Pawn center and open the "c1-h6" diagonal for his Bishop with 13 e4.

13 dxc6

This eliminates Black's Knight, which would come strongly into play in the center if White played 13 Nd2 Ne5.

13...exf3

Black recovers his Knight right away and threatens White's Queen. A very good alternative for Black would have been 13...Ng4 threatening 14...exf3 (which would attack White's Queen and threaten mate on "h2"). After 13...Ng4 the game might have continued 14 g3 exf3 15 Qxf3 Ne5 16 Qf4 (White would lose material after 16 Qe2 Bh3 17 Re1 Bg4 attacking the Queen and "f3" square a second time) Bh3 17 Rd1 Rad8 and Black is clearly better. For example, White gets into big trouble if he exchanges Rooks after 18 Rxd8 Rxd8 19 Be2 Qxc6 20 f3 Rd1+! Now if 21 Bxd1 (if White declines the Rook sacrifice with 21 Kf2 then 21...Ng4+ gives White the choice of 22 fxg4 Qg2++ or losing his Queen after 22 Qxg4 Bxg4) then 21...Qa6 (threatening 22...Qf1++) 22 c4 Qa5 (threatening 23...Qe1++) 23 Kf2 Nd3+ wins White's Queen.

Yet another good alternative for Black would have been 13...Bg4, which might have continued 14 cxb7 Qxb7 15 Qb2 Qxb2 16 Bxb2 exf3 with a good game for Black.

14 Qxf3

White gets his Queen out of attack while eliminating White's menacing Pawn.

14...Bg4

Black develops his Bishop with an attack on White's Queen.

15 Qf4

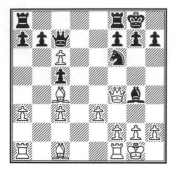

Diagram 247. Position after 15 Qf4

White gets his Queen out of attack. However, 15 Qg3 was also playable.

15...Qxc6

Black recovers his Pawn.

16 f3

White drives Black's Bishop away from its aggressive post while gaining control over "e4".

16...Be6

Black gets his Bishop out of attack while challenging White's actively posted Bishop on "c4". Black now clearly stands better in this position. This is due to having the Queenside Pawn majority, White's isolated Queenside pawns and Black having an extra piece developed. Often at the Master level two or three small advantages can be nurtured into a win!

17 Bd3?

This submissive retreat loses time and places the Bishop on a square where it is easily attacked again. White should have simplified and minimized Black's advantages by trading Bishops with 17 Bxe6 Qxe6 18 e4 Rfd8.

17...c4

Black attacks White's exposed Bishop on "d3", expands on the Queenside where he has the Queenside Pawn majority and prevents White from playing "c4".

18 Bc2

Diagram 248. Position after 18 Bc2

White gets his Bishop out of attack, maintaining it on the long "b1-h7" diagonal.

18...Nd5

Black centralizes his Knight while attacking White's Queen and isolated "c" Pawn.

19 Qh4

White gets his Queen out of attack and threatens 20 Qxh7++.

19...f5

Black blocks White's Bishop on the "b1-h7" diagonal, preventing mate on "h7". This move also hinders White from playing his natural freeing move, "e4".

20 Qe1?

White passively retreats his Queen to defend his "c" Pawn, taking her away from a far more active post on "h4". It would have been better for White to develop his Bishop to defend the Pawn with 20 Bd2. This would have also connected White's Rooks.

20...Rae8

Diagram 249. Position after 20...Rae8

Black brings his only inactive piece into play, placing his Rook on the same file as White's Queen. Also, since White would like to play "e4" and White's Pawn on "e3" is a potential target, the Rook is very effectively placed on the half-open "e" file.

21 a4

White intends to develop his Bishop to "a3" while trying to restrict the advance of Black's Queenside Pawns. See if you can find Black's best move here without looking at the next move in the game.

21...Bc8!

Black opens up his Rook on the "e" file while tying down White's Bishop to the defense of his "e" Pawn. The advantage of moving the Bishop to "c8" instead of "d7" is that from "c8" the Bishop may possibly go to "b7" if the "b" Pawn is advanced. It also doesn't block the "d" file should Black decide to reposition the Rook on "d8".

22 a5

White plays aggressively and threatens to skewer Black's Queen and Rook with 23 Ba4 (if 23...b5 then White would capture "en passant" with 24 axb6 e.p.). However, it would have been better for White to complete his minor piece development and release his Queen from the task of defending the "c" Pawn with 22 Bd2. See if you can find Black's best move here without looking at the next move in the game.

22...b5

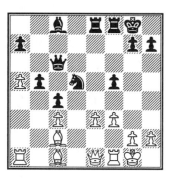

Diagram 250. Position after 22...b5

Black begins to expand on the Queenside where he has the Queenside Pawn majority and prevents White from playing 23 Ba4.

23 e4

White strikes at the center with the hopes of exchanging his weak "e" Pawn for Black's "f" Pawn and opens the "c1-h6" diagonal for the Bishop on "c1". If 23 axb6 e.p.

Black would play 23...Qxb6 24 Rb1 Qc5 with an outside passed "a" Pawn and very strong pressure on White's weak "e" Pawn.

23...fxe4

Black opens up the "f" file for his Rook and the "h3-c8" diagonal for his Bishop on "c8". Another good alternative for Black was 23...Qf6 attacking the "c" Pawn.

24 Bxe4

White recovers his Pawn and pins Black's Knight on "d5". See if you can find Black's best move here without looking at the next move in the game.

24...Bf5

Black brings his Bishop into play and attacks White's Bishop on "e4". Because of Black's threat to capture on "e4", White will be forced to give up the Bishop pair, which is his only compensation for his inferior position.

25 Bxd5+

White avoids allowing Black to capture on "e4" and breaks the pin on his Bishop.

25...Qxd5

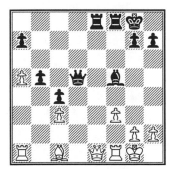

Diagram 251. Position after 25...Qxd5

Black recovers the piece and now threatens 26...Rxe1. It is funny to note that all of White's pieces are on the 1st rank while all of Black's pieces are in play!

26 Qd2

White hopes to trade Queens. Exchanging Queens would increase his drawing chances by going into an endgame with Bishops of opposite colors.

26...Bd3

Black avoids trading Queens while placing his Bishop on a very active post.

27 Re1

White gets his Rook out of attack and challenges Black's Rook on the open "e" file.

27...Qc5+

Black's idea is to make White place his King on "h1" where he is further out of play in the endgame and more exposed to possible back-rank mate threats. However, a stronger move was 27...b4! with the idea of advancing the Pawn to b3 and obtaining a strong protected passed Pawn. After 27...b4! White cannot play 28 cxb4?? because of 28...Qd4+ forking the King and Rook.

28 Kh1

Diagram 252. Position after 28 Kh1

White gets his King out of check. However, 28 Re3 was a reasonable alternative. White couldn't play 28 Qf2?? because of 28...Rxe1++.

28...Rxe1+

Black exchanges Rooks with the plan of taking control of the "e" file with his other Rook.

29 Qxe1

White recovers his Rook. Note that all of White's pieces are on the 1st rank again! See if you can find Black's best move here without looking at the next move in the game.

29...Qc6

Black covers the "e8" square so that his Rook will be protected if it shifts to the "e" file. This move also threatens a neat Rook sacrifice with 30...Rxf3! 31 gxf3? Qxf3+ 32 Kg1 Qg4+ and White must lose his Queen or be checkmated after 33 Qg3 (if 33 Kh1 then Be4+ or if 33 Kf2 then Qh4+) Qd1+ 34 Kf2 (if 34 Kg2 then Qf1++) Qe2+ 35 Kg1 Qf1++.

30 Qg3?

Diagram 253. Position after 30 Qg3

This allows Black's very strong reply. It would have been better to finally get his Bishop developed with 30 Be3. See if you can find Black's best move here without looking at the next move in the game.

30...Qf6!

Shifting the Queen to "f6" was yet another idea behind Black's 29th move. Black threatens and pins White's Pawn on "c3".

31 Bd2?

This gives up the Bishop's coverage of the important "b2" square and doesn't break the pin on White's "c" Pawn. Either 31 Ra3 (as ugly as it looks!) Re8 unpinning the "c" Pawn or 31 Bb2 b4 32 Re1 b3 (stronger than 32...bxc3 33 Ba1) setting up a blockade on the "b" file would have offered more resistance. See if you can find Black's best move here without looking at the next move in the game.

31...b4

This forces a breakthrough, creating a passed Pawn on the Queenside.

32 Bg5

This move is desperation and gives Black two connected passed Pawns. However, there was no adequate defense. If 32 Qe1 then 32...b3 33 Bc1 (White just cannot seem to keep his pieces off the 1st rank!—if 33 Qc1 then Black takes control of the "e" file with 33...Re8) Qg6 with the idea of 34...Re8 gives Black an overwhelming position.

32...Qxc3

Black wins a Pawn and now has two connected passed Pawns on the Queenside.

33 Rc1

Diagram 254. Position after 33 Rc1

White gets his Rook out of attack and attacks Black's Queen.

33...Qb2

Black's Queen gets out of attack and ties Black's Bishop down to the defense of his Rook. White has no defense against the eventual advance of Black's passed Pawns. White resigned here. One possible continuation may have been 34 Qe1 h6 35 Be3 Re8 36 Qg1 b3 37 Bd4 Qe2 followed by 38...b2.

The Double Sacrifice

Miguel Najdorf versus Hernan Salazar
Santiago, 1980

Opening: Reti

Chilean Master Hernan Salazar defeats Argentina's famous Grandmaster Miguel Najdorf with a brilliant Knight and Rook sacrifice. Soon after the sacrifices, all of Black's pieces are used in the attack on White's King and pinned Rook.

1 Nf3

Diagram 255. Position after 1 Nf3

This is known as the Reti Opening. White develops a Knight toward the center. This flexible move, which doesn't commit any Pawns, often transposes into one of many other possible openings.

1...c5

Black attacks the center with a Pawn. I usually recommend to my students that they play the flexible developing move 1...Nf6. This is so that after 2 d4 e6 3 c4 b6 they transpose into the Queen's Indian, or after 2 c4 e6 3 Nc3 Bb4 they transpose into the Nimzo-Indian after 4 d4 or English Opening after 4 Qc2. When playing an opening that may transpose into another opening it is important that you don't transpose into an opening you aren't prepared to play! Also possible was 1...d5 which may transpose into the Queen's Gambit Declined after 2 d4 Nf6 3 c4 e6 4 Nc3 Be7.

2 g3

White prepares to fianchetto his Bishop to "g2". Here 2 c4 would have transposed into the English Opening and 2 e4 would have transposed into the Sicilian Defense!

2...d5

Black places a Pawn in the center and frees his Bishop along the "h3-c8" diagonal.

3 Bg2

White completes his fianchetto, placing his Bishop on the long "h1-a8" diagonal.

3...Nc6

Black develops a Knight toward the center, supporting the possible placement of a Pawn on "e5".

4 0-0

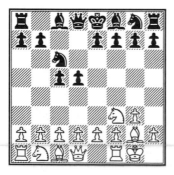

Diagram 256. Position after 4 0-0

White gets his King out of the center. White continues to maintain flexibility by delaying where he will place his Pawns in the center.

4...e6

Black reinforces his Pawn on "d5" and frees his Bishop on "f8". Other reasonable moves were 4...e5 (creating a massive Pawn center) or natural development with 4...Nf6.

5 c4

White finally places a Pawn in the center. Here 5 d3 would transpose into the King's Indian Attack. One interesting line is 5...Nf6 6 Nbd2 Be7 7 e4 b6 8 Re1 Bb7 9 e5 Nd7 10 h4 Qc7 11 Qe2 0-0-0 12 Nf1 h6 13 N1h2 Kb8 14 Bf4 Rdg8 with the idea of attacking on the Kingside with 15...g5. Also, after 5 d4, Black would transpose into a variation of the Catalan Opening after 5...Nf6.

5...Nf6

Black develops a Knight toward the center and further reinforces his Pawn on "d5". If 5...dxc4 White would easily recover his Pawn after 6 Na3.

6 cxd5

White eliminates the attack on his "c" Pawn.

6...exd5

Diagram 257. Position after 6...exd5

Black recovers his Pawn and frees his Bishop along the "h3-c8" diagonal. However, 6...Nxd5 was also playable.

7 d4

White strikes at the center with another Pawn, freeing his Queenside pieces.

7...Be7

Black develops a Bishop and prepares to castle on the Kingside. Since a good location for the Bishops on "c1" and "c8" have not yet been established, both sides will delay the development of these Bishops.

8 dxc5

White isolates Black's "d" Pawn and makes Black move his Bishop a second time to recover his Pawn. However, as compensation Black will have active pieces. Here 8 Nc3 was a good alternative.

8...Bxc5

Black recovers his Pawn and places his Bishop on the active "g1-a7" diagonal.

9 Nbd2

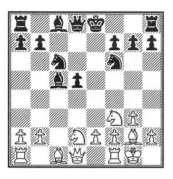

Diagram 258. Position after 9 Nbd2

White intends to maneuver his Knight to "b3" and doesn't mind temporarily blocking his Bishop on "c1". However, it would have been more active to develop a Bishop and pin Black's Knight with 9 Bg5, which might have continued 9...0-0 10 Nc3 d4 11 Bxf6 Qxf6 12 Ne4 Qe7 13 Nxc5 Qxc5 14 Rc1 Qb6 15 Qc2.

9...0-0

Black removes his King from the center and brings his Kingside Rook into play.

10 Nb3

This threatens Black's Bishop on "c5" and contests Black's control of the important "d4" square.

10...Bb6

Black gets his Bishop out of attack while keeping it well posted on the long "g1-a7" diagonal.

11 Nbd4

White blockades Black's isolated "d" Pawn. This also allows White's "b" Pawn to move and free his Bishop on the "c1-a3" diagonal.

11...Re8

Diagram 259. Position after 11...Re8

Black activates his Rook by placing it on a half-open file where it helps to control the center and puts pressure on White's "e" Pawn.

12 Nxc6?

This eliminates Black's isolated "d" Pawn and gives Black a stronger Pawn center. It would have been better for White to have continued with his plan of freeing his Bishop on the "c1-a3" diagonal with 12 b3, which might have continued 12...Ne4 13 Bb2 Bg4 14 Rc1.

12...bxc6

Black recovers his Knight.

13 b3?

White prepares to develop his Bishop to "b2" or "a3" and the Pawn on "b3" would not be threatened down the line if Black places a Rook on the "b" file. However, it would have been better for White to have played 13 Qc2 bringing his Queen into play and applying pressure along the "c" file. See if you can find Black's best move here without looking at the next move in the game.

13...Ba6

Black develops his Bishop to the long "f1-a6" diagonal and threatens White's "e" Pawn. Black stands considerably better due to his lead in development, more actively placed pieces and strong Pawn center.

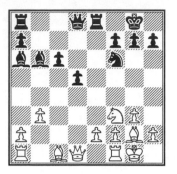

Diagram 260. Position after 13...Ba6

14 Re1

White unpins and defends his threatened "e" Pawn. See if you can find Black's best move here without looking at the next move in the game.

14...Ne4

Black takes the natural outpost for his Knight and threatens 15...Bxf2+.

15 e3

White blocks Black's Bishop's attack on the "f2" Pawn. This move weakens the white squares, but the alternative 15 Be3 would leave White with doubled isolated Pawns after 15...Bxe3 16 fxe3. See if you can find Black's best move here without looking at the next move in the game.

15...Qf6

Black brings his Queen into play, threatening White's Rook on "a1" and assisting with the build-up on the Kingside.

16 Ba3

On the surface this active developing move, which defends White's Rook on "a1", looks good. However, as Black will soon demonstrate, this move is disastrous. Even after the more passive 16 Bd2 White is in trouble after 16...g5! (threatening 17...g4) 17 h3 h5 18 g4 Bc8! If 16 Rb1 Black would play 16...d4! (this is stronger than

16...Nc3 17 Bb2) 17 Qc2 Nc3 18 Ra1 d3 19 Qb2 Rad8. See if you can find Black's best move here without looking at the next move in the game.

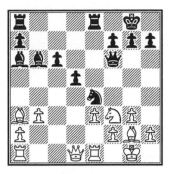

Diagram 261. Position after 16 Ba3

16...Nxf2!

This sacrifice, which exposes White's King to a powerful attack, probably hit White like a bolt from the blue.

17 Kxf2

White accepts the sacrifice, which forces Black to prove that it is sound. Refusing the sacrifice would be an admission of defeat after 17 Qc2 Rxe3 and Black is two Pawns up with a great position. See if you can find Black's best move here without looking at the next move in the game.

17...Rxe3!

Black offers a second sacrifice, which sets up a killer pin along the "g1-a7" diagonal for his Bishop. Black is now threatening 18...Rxf3++.

18 Rxe3

Due to Black's threat, White had little choice but to accept the Rook sacrifice.

18...Re8

Black brings his Rook into play while attacking White's pinned Rook on "e3".

Diagram 262. Position after 18...Re8

19 Bc1

White was faced with the decision of choosing which Rook he would lose. If White tried hiding his King with 19 Kg1 then Black would play 19...Rxe3 20 Kh1 Be2 and White will be hopelessly behind in material.

19...Qxa1

Black recovers his Rook while threatening 20...Bxe3+ (due to the pin on White's Bishop on "c1") and 20...Qxa2+.

20 Qc2

White unpins his Bishop on "c1", defends his Pawn on "a2" and attacks Black's unprotected Pawn on "c6". Though this is certainly White's best move in the situation, his game is hopelessly lost. See if you can find Black's best move here without looking at the next move in the game.

20...Bd3!

This is the key move in the position—it drives White's Queen away from a good defensive square.

21 Qxc6?

Instead of going Pawn grabbing White could have offered better resistance with 21 Qxd3 Qxc1 22 Nd4 Qb2+ 23 Ke1 Rd8 24 Nc2 Bxe3 25 Nxe3 Qxa2. White would have two minor pieces for a rook and three pawns, which would be a slow but sure

win for Black with correct play. See if you can find Black's best move here without looking at the next move in the game.

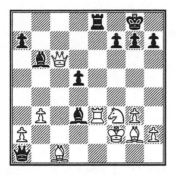

Diagram 263. Position after 21 Qxc6

21...Rxe3!

White resigned here. If White played 22 Qc8+ then Black has a discovered check with the Bishop on "b6" after 22...Re8+. If White played 22 Bxe3 then Black would have played 22...Qxa2+ 23 Kg1 Bxe3+ 24 Kh1 Qb1+.

Wonder Bishops

Perry Youngworth versus Robert Snyder
Santa Monica, 1975

Opening: English

The effective use of the Bishop pair is clearly demonstrated in this game. After the game several spectators gave applause and came over to commend my use of what one of them called "wonder Bishops".

1 c4

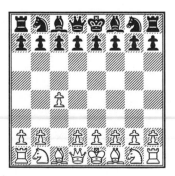

Diagram 264. Position after 1 c4

This is known as the English Opening. White uses a Pawn to attack the center. This flexible move, like that of the Reti Opening, often transposes into one of many possible openings.

1...Nf6

This is Black's most flexible move. He develops a Knight toward the center and prevents an immediate 2 e4.

2 Nc3

White also develops a Knight toward the center and supports the possible posting of a Pawn on "e4".

2...e6

Black frees his Bishop along the "a3-f8" diagonal and prepares support for a future "d5".

3 g3

Diagram 265. Position after 3 g3

White prepares to fianchetto his Bishop to "g2". Here White had a variety of choices. With 3 d4 Bb4 he transposes into the Nimzo-Indian Defense or with 3 d4 d5 hc transposes into the Queen's Gambit Declined. Very aggressive would be 3 e4 which is best met by 3...d5 4 e5 d4 5 exf6 dxc3 6 bxc3 Qxf6 7 d4 e5 with an even game.

3...Bb4

Black develops his Bishop to an active post, which attacks White's Knight and prepares to castle. The moves 3...c5 or 3...d5 were also playable.

4 Bg2

White completes his fianchetto, placing his Bishop on the long "h1-a8" diagonal. Here White could again have transposed into a variation of the Nimzo-Indian Defense with 4 d4. After 4 d4 one possible continuation is 4...0-0 5 Bg2 d5 6 Nf3 dxc4 7 0-0 Nc6 8 Qa4 Nd5 9 Qc2 Be7.

4...0-0

Black removes his King from the center early in the opening.

5 Nf3

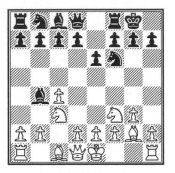

Diagram 266. Position after 5 Nf3

White develops a Knight toward the center and clears the way for castling.

5...d5

Black aggressively places a Pawn in the center, frees his Queenside pieces and attacks White's unprotected "c" Pawn.

6 cxd5

White gets his Pawn out of attack by exchanging it for Black's Pawn. Other possibilities for White were 6 a3 Be7 7 d4 dxc4 8 Ne5 c5 9 dxc5 Qc7, or 6 d4 dxc4 7 0-0 Nc6.

6...exd5

Black recovers his Pawn while maintaining a Pawn in the center and opening the "h3-c8" diagonal for his Bishop. Black now threatens to drive White's Knight away from "c3" and gain more space in the center with 7...d4.

7 d4

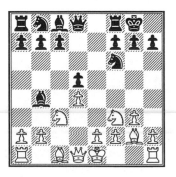

Diagram 267. Position after 7 d4

White occupies the center with a Pawn, frees his Bishop on "c1" and prevents Black from playing 7...d4.

7...c6

This is a move with many good ideas behind it. Black reinforces the defense of his "d" Pawn, restricts White's use of the half-open "c" file and gives his Queen more options by opening the "a5-d8" diagonal. Also, in the event that Black's Bishop retreats to "d6", the Pawn on "c6" will prevent White from attacking the Bishop with Nb5.

8 0-0

White removes his King from the center.

8...Re8

Black places his Rook on the half-open center file and puts pressure on White's "e" Pawn.

9 Bd2

This is a passive location for the Bishop. It would have been stronger to develop it to a more active diagonal with 9 Bf4 or to delay its development and bring the Queen into play with 9 Qc2.

9...Nbd7

Black develops his Knight to its most active available square. Black doesn't mind blocking his Bishop on "c8" since the Knight's post on "d7" is only temporary.

10 Rc1

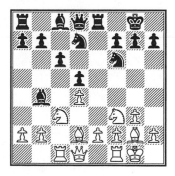

Diagram 268. Position after 10 Rc1

White places his Rook on the half-open "c" file. However, the Rook will not be of much use on this file. It would have been more effective for White to play 10 Re1 to aid in the support of his "e" Pawn. As a general rule *"Don't place a Rook on an open*

*or half-open file just for the sake of it. The Rook should have either one or more poten-
tial squares to penetrate, be defending or attacking a piece or, in some way, applying
pressure on the opponent."*

10...Nb6

Black maneuvers his Knight toward the Queenside where it can be posted on "c4".
This move also reopens the "h3-c8" diagonal for Black's undeveloped Bishop on "c8".

11 Ne5

White posts his Knight aggressively on its natural outpost and prevents Black's
Knight from immediately going to "c4".

11...Ng4

Black aggressively challenges White's actively posted Knight on "e5". However, a
strategic retreat attacking White's Knight on "e5" with 11...Bd6 12 Bf4 Bf5 was even
stronger.

12 e4?

This attack in the center is premature and leads to unfavorable exchanges for
White. Because of the discovered attack by White's Queen he threatens to win Black's
Knight with 13 Nxg4. White should have repositioned his Knight, attacking Black's
Bishop on "b4", with 12 Nd3. Though after 12 Nd3 Bd6 Black stands slightly better.

12...Nxe5

Black eliminates the threat on his Knight while exchanging it for White's actively
posted Knight.

13 dxe5

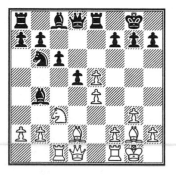

Diagram 269. Position after 13 dxe5

White recovers his Knight.

13...dxe4

Black eliminates the pressure on his "d" Pawn by exchanging it for White's Pawn. Black can then focus on taking advantage of Black's weak Pawn on "e5".

14 Bxe4

White decides to immediately eliminate Black's "e" Pawn. However, there shouldn't have been any rush. White's best move was 14 Re1 (planning to meet 14...Nc4? with 15 Rxe4), which still leaves Black with a nice advantage after 14...e3 15 Bxe3 Qxd1 16 Rcxd1 Nc4 17 Bc1 h6. Another interesting move for White was to defend his Pawn on "e5" with 14 Bf4. However, after 14 Bf4 Black gets a great game with 14...Qxd1 15 Rfxd1 Bxc3 16 Rxc3 Nd5.

14...Rxe5

Black wins a Pawn. Another possibility, which would leave Black ahead by a Pawn with White having some compensation, was 14...Nc4 15 Bf4 Qxd1 16 Rfxd1 Nxb2 17 Rd2 Nc4 18 Rd4 Bxc3 19 Rxc3 Nb6.

15 Qe2?

White places his Queen on the same file as Black's Rook. As a result White placed a pin on his own Bishop. The only reason for this move must have been White's threat of 16 Bxh7+ Kxh7 17 Qxe5 Qxd2 18 Qe4+ Kg8 19 Qxb4. As a general rule *"Do not make an inferior move based on the hope that your opponent will overlook a threat that can easily be stopped."* In other words, *"Hoping your opponent will fall for a trap instead of looking for and finding the best reply will prove to be unproductive in the long run."*

White's best move was 15 Qc2 bringing the Queen to a more active square, connecting his Rooks and threatening 16 Bxh7+. However, after 15 Qc2 f5 White still wouldn't have had enough compensation for the Pawn he lost.

See if you can find Black's best move here without looking at the next move in the game.

15...f5

Diagram 270. Position after 15...f5

Black prevents White's threat of 16 Bxh7+ while attacking and threatening White's pinned Bishop. This will force White to trade Queens and give Black a superior position.

16 Qd3

This is the only move to prevent the loss of more material. White unpins his Bishop and challenges Black's unprotected Queen. If 16 Bd5+ then 16...Rxd5 17 Nxd5 Nxd5 18 Bxb4 Nxb4 and Black has two minor pieces and a Pawn for a Rook.

16...Qxd3

Black doesn't mind trading Queens and getting a nice position since he is a Pawn ahead. Another good alternative for Black was to develop and defend his Queen with 16...Be6. After 16...Be6 the game might have continued 17 Qxd8 Rxd8 18 Bg5 Re8 and Black is up a Pawn with a superior position.

17 Bxd3

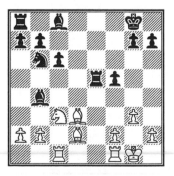

Diagram 271. Position after 17 Bxd3

White recovers his Queen.

See if you can find Black's best move here without looking at the next move in the game.

17...Re8!

Black repositions his Rook before developing his Bishop to "e6", which would cut off the Rook's retreat. Black now threatens to skewer White's Bishops and win a piece with 18...Rd8.

18 Be3

White removes a Bishop from the "d" file to avoid the skewer. The Bishop is actively posted on "e3" and blocks the Black Rook on the "e" file.

See if you can find Black's best move here without looking at the next move in the game.

18...Be6

Black finally gets his Bishop developed! This will allow Black to get his Rook on "a8" into play and puts pressure on White's "a" Pawn.

19 Bb1?

Diagram 272. Position after 19 Bb1

White passively retreats his Bishop to aid in the defense of his "a" Pawn. It would have been better to get the Pawn off of "a2" and attack Black's Bishop with 19 a3. After 19 a3 Black's best move would be 19...Be7 with the idea of moving the Bishop to "f6" on the long "a1-h8" diagonal and possibly posting the Knight on "c4".

See if you can find Black's best move here without looking at the next move in the game.

19...Nc4

This is an awesome post for the Knight. It attacks White's unprotected "b" Pawn and Bishop on "e3".

20 Nd1

White retreats his Knight to defend his Pawn on "b2" and Bishop on "e3".

20...Nxe3

In addition to being a Pawn up with a nice position, Black now gets the Bishop pair. Another good way to get the Bishop pair was 20...Nd2 21 Bxd2 Bxd2 22 Rc2 Rad8.

21 Nxe3

White recovers his piece and attacks Black's "f" Pawn a second time. White avoided playing 21 fxe3, which would have given him an isolated "e" Pawn on an open file.

21...g6

Diagram 273. Position after 21...g6

Black defends his "f" Pawn and opens up "g7" for possible use by his Bishop.

22 Nc4

White hopes to make his Knight more active by bringing it to attack the dark squares on the Queenside and in the center.

22...Bd5

Black centralizes his Bishop and opens up the "e" file for his Rook to take advantage of White's white square weaknesses on the Kingside. A good alternative for Black was to bring his inactive Rook into play on the open "d" file with 22...Rad8.

23 a3

White attacks and drives Black's aggressively posted Bishop away.

23...Bf8

Black gets his Bishop out of attack by placing it where it can be repositioned on either the "a1-h8" or "c1-h6" diagonal.

24 Na5

Diagram 274. Position after 24 Na5

White tries to get counterplay on the Queenside by attacking Black's Pawn on "b7".

See if you can find Black's best move here without looking at the next move in the game.

24...Bg7

For now Black ignores the threat on his "b" Pawn and creates a greater threat by bringing his Bishop into play on the long "a1-h8" diagonal. Black threatens to play 25...Bxb2 forking White's Rook and "a" Pawn.

25 Rc2

White defends his threatened Pawn on "b2".

25...Re7

Black defends his Pawn on "b7" and allows for the possibility of doubling his Rooks on a central file.

26 b4

Diagram 275. Position after 26 b4

White relieves the necessity for his Rook to defend his "b" Pawn and continues with his plan to get counterplay on the Queenside. This move also gives White the possibility of moving his inactive Bishop to "a2" to exchange it for Black's strongly centralized Bishop on "d5".

26...Rc8

Black's idea is to defend his "c" Pawn a second time so that he can move his Pawn to "b6" to drive away White's aggressively posted Knight. However, it will soon become apparent that the Rook belongs on the "e" file.

It would have been better to play 26...Kf8 to avoid having to exchange Bishops on the "a2-g8" diagonal. After 26...Kf8 Black would meet 27 Ba2 with 27...Bf3.

27 Rd1

White brings his inactive Rook into play with the threat of 28 Rxd5 Re1+ 29 Kg2 Rxb1 30 Rd7 and White will recover his Pawn with a great position. However, White missed his opportunity to force a trade of Bishops with 27 Ba2 Bxa2 28 Rxa2. Although Black would still have a won game, Black's positional advantage wouldn't have been as great. Now the effective use of the Bishop pair will come to light, showing its dominance over a Bishop and a Knight!

27...Rce8

This move unpins Black's "c" Pawn and doubles Black's Rooks on the open "e" file. Because White's Rook was moved from "f1" to "d1", Black now threatens 28...Re1+ 29 Rxe1 Rxe1++.

28 Kf1

Diagram 276. Position after 28 Kf1

White's King defends the "e1" square against the mate threat.

See if you can find Black's best move here without looking at the next move in the game.

28...Bf3!

Black prevents White from forcing a trade of Bishops with 29 Ba2 and prevents White from playing 29 f4 (opening up an escape square for White's King on "f2" and blocking the possible use of the "c1-h6" diagonal by Black's Bishop). This move, which cramps White, also threatens White's Rook on "d1".

29 Ba2+

White places his Bishop on a more active diagonal and opens up more squares for White's Rook on the 1st rank.

29...Kf8

Black gets his King out of check by moving him to where he will be most active.

30 Rdc1

Diagram 277. Position after 30 Rdc1

White gets his Rook out of attack, delaying the loss of more material as long as possible. If White played 30 Rb1 then 30...Be4 wins the exchange.

See if you can find Black's best move here without looking at the next move in the game.

30...Bh6!

Black's Bishop attacks White's Rook on "c1", which forces the win of more material.

31 Ra1

White gets his Rook out of attack and delays the loss of material.

31...f4

Black's idea is to possibly use his "f" Pawn on "f3" and set up a mate. However, 31...Be4 was more direct. After 31...Be4 Black will force at least the win of the ex-

change (*i.e.* if 32 Rc4 then 32...Bd3+, if 32 Rc3 or 32 Rb2 then 32...Bg7, if 32 Rc5 then 32...b6, and finally if 32 Re2?? then 32...Bd3).

32 Nc4

It is too late for White to try to bring his Knight to the rescue. However, White's situation was hopeless. If White opened up "a2" for use by his Rooks with 32 Bb3, then one possible continuation might have been 32...Be4 33 Rca2 Bg7 34 Rd1 Bf3 35 Rc1 Bc3!, forcing the win of more material due to the threat of 36...Re1+ 37 Rxe1 Rxe1++. If White had played 32 gxf4 then Black wins more material with 32...Be4 33 Rd2 Bxf4 34 Rdd1 (if 34 Rd4 then 34...Be5) Bc2 35 Rd4 Be5.

32...Be4

Diagram 278. Position after 32 Be4

Black attacks White's Rook on "c2" forcing the win of more material. White resigned here. If White played 33 Rd2 or 33 Rcc1 then Black could have played 33...fxg3 with a discovered attack by the Bishop on "h6" on White's Rook. If White played 33 Rc3 or 33 Rb2 then Black could have skewered White's Rooks with 33...Bg7. And finally, if White played 33 Re2 Black wins the Rook immediately with 33...Bd3. It is no wonder why this game is called "Wonder Bishops"!

About the Author

Robert M. Snyder is a highly regarded chess educator and well-known personality in scholastic chess circles. He has introduced chess to more than 160,000 Elementary and Junior High School students through his presentations. His students have won first place 35 times (a national record) as individuals in championship sections at the National Scholastic Championships. His teams have won 10 National Scholastic Championships.

At the age of twelve, Mr. Snyder learned how to play chess. By the time he was eighteen, he earned the title of National Chess Master. In 1973 he became champion of the Western United States. Mr. Snyder represented the United States on the Correspondence Olympic Team, qualified for the semifinals of the World Correspondence Championships and earned an International rating of 2405.

In 1983 he founded the "Chess For Juniors" club, which is now based in Fort Collins, Colorado. He currently trains about 60 local students at the club and about 30 students on the Internet. He has written articles for *Chess Life* and *School Mates* magazines and is the author of *Chess For Juniors* and *The Snyder Sicilian*.